This book is a companion volume to the Royal Economic Society edition of *The Works and Correspondence of David Ricardo*, edited by Piero Sraffa with the collaboration of Maurice Dobb. It completes the record on Ricardian value theory by showing Ricardo's reaction to Malthus's pamphlet *The Measure of Value Stated and Illustrated* of 1823. Ricardo's Notes are, in Sraffa's words, 'the only considerable item' not appearing in the Royal Economic Society edition of his works. In addition, the recent publication by Cambridge of the variorum edition of Malthus's *Principles of Political Economy*, edited by J. M. Pullen, makes it possible to understand Malthus's pamphlet as an intermediate step between the 1820 and 1836 editions of the *Principles*.

In his introduction Pier Luigi Porta highlights the place of these Notes in the development of Ricardo's thinking. When taken with Ricardo's paper on 'Absolute Value and Exchangeable Value', these Notes provide the essentials of Ricardian value theory. The style of the present edition conforms throughout with Volume II (*Notes on Malthus*) of the Sraffa edition of Ricardo's *Works*.

David Ricardo: Notes on Malthus's 'Measure of Value'

David Ricardo: Notes on Malthus's 'Measure of Value'

Edited by
PIER LUIGI PORTA

The right of the University of Cambridge to print and sell all manner of books was granted by Henry VIII in 1534. The University has printed and published continuously since 1584.

CAMBRIDGE UNIVERSITY PRESS

CAMBRIDGE
NEW YORK PORT CHESTER
MELBOURNE SYDNEY

Published by the Press Syndicate of the University of Cambridge
The Pitt Building, Trumpington Street, Cambridge CB2 1RP
40 West 20th Street, New York, NY 10011-4211, USA
10 Stamford Road, Oakleigh, Victoria 3166, Australia

First published 1992

Printed in Great Britain at the University Press, Cambridge

British Library cataloguing in publication data

17 July, 1990
Ricardo, David 1772–1823
Notes on Malthus's 'Measure of Value'.
1. Economics. Theories of Malthus, T. R. (Thomas Robert), 1766–1836
I. Title II. Porta, Pier Luigi
III Malthus, T. R. (Thomas Robert) 1766–1834. Measure of value stated and illustrated . . .
330.153

Library of Congress cataloguing in publication data applied for

ISBN 0 521 402 98 0 hardback

CE

Contents

Introduction *page* ix

'The Measure of Value Stated and Illustrated', with Ricardo's Notes on the text 1

Appendix: a letter of J. Mill to J. R. McCulloch 57

Index 60

Introduction

The origin of Ricardo's Notes

The Measure of Value Stated and Illustrated With an Application of It to the Alterations in the Value of the English Currency Since 1790 by Thomas Robert Malthus appeared in print in April 1823.[1] Soon after its publication, Ricardo recorded a critical reaction in a letter to Malthus of 29 April: 'After the most attentive consideration which I can give to your book, I cannot agree with you in considering labour, in the sense in which you use it, as a good measure of value.' Malthus's sense is the quantity of labour commodities will command as opposed to the quantity of labour which is employed upon them.[2] With this statement Ricardo's correspondence reverted to the discussion of value after over two years' interval, the measure of value becoming the dominant issue in his letters during the summer of 1823, the last months of his life.[3] Reading Malthus's pamphlet, therefore, marked the beginning of a new train of reflection on a problem which had preoccupied Ricardo in particular during the latter half of 1820, while he was revising his own *Principles* for the third edition published in the spring of 1821, and

[1] London: John Murray. Advertised as 'Published this day' in the *Morning Chronicle*, 24 April 1823; no indication of price. Priced at 3s. 6d. in the *Monthly Literary Advertiser*, 10 May 1823.

[2] Ricardo's letter 523 in *The Works and Correspondence of David Ricardo*, eleven volumes, edited by Piero Sraffa with the collaboration of M. H. Dobb, Cambridge University Press (henceforth quoted as *Works*), vol. IX, p. 280. For Malthus's sense, cp. also Malthus's *Measure of Value*, pp. v, 13–16; below, pp. 6, 16–17.

[3] Ricardo died on 11 September 1823 and his last letter (to Mill) was of 5 September. Before April 1823 the last letter in which Ricardo dealt extensively with value was to McCulloch, 29 January 1821 (letter 418, *Works*, vol. VIII, pp. 342–5).

while, at the same time, he was also compiling his extensive commentary on Malthus's *Principles*.[4]

The significance of Ricardo's final reflections on value could not be fully appreciated before the appearance of Piero Sraffa's edition of Ricardo's works. In particular, the discovery, in 1943, of the 'Mill–Ricardo Papers' brought to light Ricardo's very last paper which – according to Sraffa – 'has importance since it develops an idea which existed previously in Ricardo's writings only in occasional hints and allusions: namely, the notion of a real or absolute value underlying and contrasted with exchangeable or relative value'.[5] Among the same set of papers a further item was found, namely a series of seventeen rough Notes on Malthus's pamphlet on the *Measure of Value*. Curiously, however, these Notes were not included in the Sraffa edition, where they are described as 'the only considerable item' left behind. They were first published in Padua by a leading economic journal in Italy.[6]

Some account of the discovery of the 'Mill–Ricardo Papers' appears in the General Preface to the *Works* of Ricardo (vol. I, p. ix), and their contents are described in volume X of Ricardo's *Works* (pp. 391–2). Besides containing the whole series of Ricardo's letters to James Mill, long believed to have been lost, the 'Mill–Ricardo Papers' include 'a number of manuscripts which appear to have been sent to James Mill at Ricardo's death, no doubt with a view to his deciding which were suitable for publication'.[7] The editor of Ricardo's *Works*, in his note on Ricardo's last writings on value (vol. IV, pp. 358–9), further observes that a hint of the existence of these writings, in McCulloch's *Life and Writings of David Ricardo*, had been completely

[4] *Notes on Malthus's Principles of Political Economy*, in *Works*, vol. II. On Ricardo's concern with value, see *Works*, vol. I, Introduction, pp. xxx and ff.

[5] *Works*, vol. IV, p. 359. Ricardo's last paper is published in *Works*, vol. IV, pp. 361–97 (rough draft) and 398–412 (later version), with two minor additions on pp. 396–7 and 399, fn.), under the title of 'Absolute Value and Exchangeable Value'. The significance of the concept of 'absolute value' is also emphasized by the Sraffa edition in *Works*, vol. I, pp. xliii and xlv–xlvii.

[6] See *Rivista Internazionale di Scienze Economiche e Commerciali-International Review of Economics and Business*, vol. XXVI (1979), pp. 7–35.

The proper place for Ricardo's Notes should have been in *Works*, vol. IV, first published in 1951, among the 'Notes from Ricardo's Manuscripts 1818–23', immediately *after* the Notes on Blake and *before* 'Absolute Value and Exchangeable Value'. They are, in fact, only described in vol. X, app. B, containing the final survey of Ricardo's manuscripts, which appeared four years later, in 1955 (see in particular ibid., p. 392). It is curious that James Mill – almost certainly independently of Ricardo – left a series of notes on Malthus's 1823 value pamphlet. The MS of Mill's Notes belongs to the 'Mill-Taylor Collection', vol. LIX, fol. 14 at the London School of Economics. A reference to this MS is made in D. Winch (ed.), *Selected Economic Writings of James Mill* (Edinburgh, 1966), p. 191, fn.

[7] *Works*, vol. X, p. 391.

overlooked. The result of Ricardo's reconsideration on value, Sraffa adds, 'must have been sent to Mill after Ricardo's death, together with the *Plan for the National Bank*; but unlike the latter it was apparently regarded by Mill as not suitable for publication'.

A few pieces of information can now be added to this story. In particular, we are now able to confirm the above conjectures as a result of a newly published letter from Mill to McCulloch of 10 January 1824 which is appended to the present volume.[8]

> I have been to Brighton to see Mrs. Ricardo – Mill writes – and have seen all the MSS they had there. The plan for the Bank seems to have received his last hand; and as Mr. Moses [David's brother], to whom all the papers are confided, is anxious for its publication, and I see no reason against it, this will soon appear. You already know pretty well what it is. There is a good deal written on the subject of value, but rather in scraps, and as thoughts put down as they were excogitated, than in a form for the public.

Besides hinting at the existence of writings on value, this letter indicates that Mill was advising Moses Ricardo on how to deal with David's literary remains. While the plan for the Bank was, in fact, soon to appear in print,[9] Ricardo's MSS on value must have subsequently been passed on to James Mill. He evidently regarded them as unsuitable for publication:

> I do not find any thing new – he went on in his letter to McCulloch – any thing different from the ideas we have heard him throw out. I think it is possible that in some of his letters to you, or to Malthus, his thoughts may be put in a better form, than in the papers I have seen. If so, they ought to be made use of, at least in detailed account of his life.[10]

A few particulars can also be added to Sraffa's own account of the discovery of the 'Mill–Ricardo Papers' (*Works*, vol. I, p. ix and vol. X, p. 391) through the courtesy of the Royal Economic Society, which has

[8] MS in the University of London Library, AL 187/25. This letter also confirms Sraffa's conjecture about the authorship of the anonymous 'Memoir of Ricardo [by one of his brothers]', the earliest biographical sketch of David Ricardo. Cp. *Works*, vol. X, pp. 14–15.

[9] *Plan for the Establishment of a National Bank*, by (the late) David Ricardo, Esq., MP, 1824. Cp. *Works*, vol. IV, pp. 276–97.

[10] Mill's opinion was probably responsible for McCulloch's change of emphasis on those papers through successive versions of his *Life and Writings of David Ricardo*. Sraffa, in particular, notes that McCulloch drops the mention of Ricardo's inquiry on absolute and exchangeable value (*Works*, vol. IV, p. 358, text and note 2). On the other hand Mill's idea of making use of the correspondence was almost entirely ignored by McCulloch in his edition of Ricardo's *Works* published in 1846. It is perhaps curious that Mill does not mention the *Notes on Malthus* of 1820 in this letter. It may be conjectured that they had been seen by Mill *before* Ricardo's death, so that there was no longer any question at that stage about their publication. See also *Works*, vol. II, pp. xi–xii, xiv, xvi.

now given access to the relevant documents preserved among the 'Keynes Papers'. The Mill–Ricardo Papers were found at the beginning of July 1943 in Ireland through the good offices of Professor Hayek, who was then working on the biography of John Stuart Mill. The discovery occurred in the house of Mr F. E. Cairnes, the son of John Elliot, the economist and close friend of John Stuart Mill. The find was described in a letter of Mr C. K. Mill from Dublin of 2 July 1943. This stated that an 'old box' had just been discovered with 'a number of letters which may be of interest to you. They have not yet been sorted out, but from a first inspection they appear to contain a beautifully written manuscript by Ricardo, a few letters between him and James Mill . . . When these are sorted out I shall pass them on to Professor O'Brien.'[11] The letter was addressed to 'Professor F. A. Hayek, The London School of Economics and Political Science, The Hostel, Peterhouse, Cambridge'.[12] Piero Sraffa immediately prepared a copy of this letter and sent it to Keynes in London. 'My dear Maynard', he wrote on 5 July, 'this is the most sensational news there has ever been about Ricardo. *His letters to Mill have been found!* And a MS by Ricardo in addition.'[13] Both Professor George O'Brien and Lord Keynes compared this find with the famous discovery of James Boswell's MSS diaries, which had occurred in Ireland in the inter-war years, and had aroused an immense stir.[14]

The main items on value which came to light among the papers are the following: (1) a draft of the paper on 'Absolute Value and Exchangeable Value', (2) an unfinished later version of the same paper, (3) a series of rough

[11] Letter of Mr C. K. Mill, a son-in-law of Mr F. E. Cairnes, to Professor Hayek. Copy in 'Keynes Papers' 1, (quoted in *Opere di David Ricardo* (Turin: Utet, 1983), p. 84.

[12] The London School had moved to Cambridge during the war.

[13] MS in 'Keynes Papers' (quoted in *Opere di David Ricardo*): 'The enclosed copy – Sraffa adds – of a letter received today by Hayek from C. K. Mill, of Dublin, tells its own story . . . [T]his letter of Mill is in reply to one of Hayek in which he told him that I was editing Ricardo for the R.E.S. and was anxious to find these letters, and enquired on my behalf.' Hayek's letter has not been found. However, the originals of the new materials may not have reached Piero Sraffa until after the war. A hint of this is given also by Professor Hayek, who, in a private letter of 29 June 1979, from Obergurgl, Tyrol, writes to the present editor: 'All I clearly remember is that when later, almost certainly when I gave the Finlay Lecture at the University of Dublin in December 1945, Sraffa asked me to bring some papers kept there for him and which he did not wish to entrust to the post.'

[14] Keynes had written to O'Brien at Sraffa's suggestion: 'It would be tactful to write, at the same time, to O'Brien, who has made the discovery and been helpful to Hayek: so as to avoid the impression that we are stealing a march on him, and the danger of a competitive situation arising, as it happened with Hollander.' Letter of 5 July 1943 (quoted in *Opere di David Ricardo*); cp. also P. L. Porta, 'How Piero Sraffa Took up the Editorship of David Ricardo's Works and Correspondence', *The History of Economics Society Bulletin*, VIII (1986), p. 35, n. 1.

Notes on Malthus's *Measure of Value*. All these MSS are now in the possession of the University Library at Cambridge.[15]

The Notes were evidently drafted by Ricardo on reading and studying Malthus's new pamphlet and the MS consists of fourteen pages in Ricardo's hand; it can be dated from the fact that two pages are written on the back of two letters addressed to Ricardo, postmarked 7 April and 7 May 1823. Some of the Notes are echoed by Ricardo's letter to Malthus of 29 April 1823.

The Notes and the debate on value between Malthus and Ricardo

Ricardo's *Notes on Malthus's 'Measure of Value'* contain a remarkable statement of one aspect of Ricardo's thinking on value. Together with the better-known paper on 'Absolute Value and Exchangeable Value', they can be considered as providing the essentials of the debate on value from the Ricardian standpoint. A brief survey of Ricardo's discussions with Malthus on value, particularly after the publication of Malthus's *Principles* in 1820, is a necessary preliminary to any understanding of the place which the present Notes occupy within the last stage of Ricardo's thinking.

Malthus himself effectively summarized the general terms of his difference with Ricardo in a *Quarterly Review* article of January 1824:

> The new school [i.e. the Ricardians] suppose that the mass of commodities obtained by the same quantity of labour remains always substantially of the same value, and that the variations of profits are determined by the variations in the value of this same quantity of labour: while Adam Smith and Mr. Malthus suppose that the value of the same quantity of labour remains substantially the same, and that the variations of profits are determined by the variations in the value of the commodities produced by this same quantity of labour. In the one case, the varying value of labour is considered as the great moving principle in the progress of wealth; in the other, the varying value of the *produce* of labour.[16]

In chapter 2 of his *Principles* ('On the Nature and Measures of Value') Malthus devoted two sections (IV and V) to a detailed criticism of Ricardo's labour-embodied measure of value.[17] In a further section (VI) he went on to

[15] UL Catalogue: MSS Add. 7510. I.

[16] *The Quarterly Review*, vol. XXX, no. LX, January 1824, p. 332; cp. also Pullen's Introduction to the variorum edition of Malthus's *Principles* (see below, fn. 17), vol. I, p. xlviii, fn. 16.

[17] *Principles of Political Economy Considered With a View to Their Practical Application*, variorum edition, edited by John M. Pullen, Cambridge University Press, two vols., 1989. The first edition, here referred to, was originally published by John Murray in 1820, while the second edition appeared posthumously in 1836.

recommend labour commanded as a measure of value.[18] Ricardo's response was twofold. In the first place he emphasized the invariable character which any measure of value must possess; secondly, he allowed that perfect invariability is conceptually unattainable. The first argument provides the original basis for Ricardo's choice of embodied labour as the measure of value, which – combined with the principle of diminishing returns – provides the whole foundation of his system. This contention is especially insisted upon throughout the *Notes on Malthus*, the present Notes providing a brief sequel to them in this respect. Ricardo's first and main criticism of Malthus's measure of value is that the latter has no basis and is entirely *arbitrary*. The second argument was developed in the third edition of the *Principles* – after being touched upon in the *Notes on Malthus* – and was finally taken up in Ricardo's last paper on 'Absolute Value and Exchangeable Value'. It leads to an increasing emphasis on the *impossibility* of attaining a perfect measure. Ricardo became convinced that all that can be done is choose among avowedly imperfect special cases: Malthus's measure provided one such case. Though in principle no more subject to criticism than any other special case, Ricardo came to regard that as an *extreme* case.[19]

In what follows the two arguments in Ricardo's response on value, as outlined above, will be taken up in turn. In general terms, Ricardo's commentary maintains a sharply critical stand on Malthus's pamphlet and on the measure of value proposed in it. Ricardo's attitude is perfectly in line with the tone and argument of his *Notes on Malthus's 'Principles'* of 1820. At the time of the present commentary he also writes to McCulloch:

[18] Cp. Malthus's *Principles*, pp. 118–19, cp. Pullen edn, vol. I, pp. 118–19. The value of an object must be estimated by the 'quantity of labour . . . which it can command'. This is the 'sense in which [labour] is most frequently applied by Adam Smith' and provides 'unquestionably the best' measure of value. Cp. also *Works*, vol. II, p. 89.

[19] On Malthus's side, the present pamphlet is a by-product of Malthus's work on a second edition of his *Principles*. It must be recalled that, soon after the publication of the *Principles* in 1820 and the ensuing debates with Ricardo, Malthus conceived the plan of a second edition of his book (cp. *Principles*, Pullen edn, Introd. to vol. I, pp. xxxvi ff. and *Works*, vol. II, p. xi). The working copy of his *Principles* (1st edn) has been preserved: those marginal annotations and insertions, which affect the chapter on measures of value, are of special interest in the present context and bear strong connections with the pamphlet commented on by Ricardo in the present Notes. Such insertions are included in the Pullen edition of Malthus's *Principles* under the symbol MR, 'Manuscript Revisions' (vol. II: see in part. 1.60a, 1.73b, 1.85c, 1.91e, 1.101d, 1.110a through i, 1.111a through f, 1.118d and 1.121l; see also vol. I, pp. xxxvii ff., where MR are discussed and cp. *Works*, vol. II, esp. pp. xii–xiv and xi). On the strong connections between Malthus's 'Manuscript Revisions' and the present pamphlet, see also *Principles*, Pullen edn, Introd. to vol. I, pp. xliii, xliv (text and fn. 3); and P. James *Population Malthus. His Life and Times*, (London: Routledge, 1979), chapter 9, par. vi, esp. pp. 317–18. A hint to the effect that Malthus's work on revision was the origin of the present pamphlet on the measure of value is given by Malthus himself in the text, pp. 60–1 (below, pp. 45–6).

> Have you seen Mr. Malthus book on the measure of value? His arguments appear to me fallacious from beginning to end – he would have done much better to rest his defence of the standard he had chosen upon the old arguments in its favor, which I think unsatisfactory, but those which he now uses are delusive and are scarcely to be understood.[20]

To this McCulloch replies: 'Though he should gain no other palm, he must be allowed praise for having rendered himself so very unintelligible.'[21]

It is easily observed that the mentioned twofold aspect of Ricardo's position on the issue of value has a straightforward correspondence with his double approach to Malthus's measure of value. While, in one sense, the constructive side of Malthus's argument, i.e. the labour commanded measure of value, can – in Ricardo's view – be readily dismissed as arbitrary, in another sense the very same argument becomes an intriguing counterexample to Ricardo's original proposition that 'no commodities whatever are raised in absolute price, merely because wages rise'. The latter proposition makes its appearance in the first edition of Ricardo's *Principles*, where it is meant to support the fundamental Ricardian tenet – rather bluntly stated in the first section heading of the second edition – that 'the value of a commodity . . . depends on the relative quantity of labour which is necessary for its production, and not on the greater or less compensation which is paid for that labour'.[22] Thus, it is the peculiar combination of the two distinct sides of Malthus's argument – or, rather, of Ricardo's double approach to it – which

[20] 3 May 1823 (*Works*, vol. IX, p. 287).

[21] 11 May 1823 (*Works*, vol. IX, p. 290). In a letter to Mill Ricardo notes: 'I am often puzzled to find any connection between the premises and conclusions of his propositions' (ibid., p. 329). To this Mill replies triumphantly: 'Poor Malthus, and his Measure of Value! I am more and more satisfied that your account of the matter, which both McCulloch and myself have adopted, is the true exposition' (ibid., p. 334). Other reactions to Malthus's measure of value pamphlet are reported by James, *Population Malthus*, p. 320 and in *Principles*, Pullen edn, Introd. to vol. I, p. xliv. Particularly against Bailey's criticisms, Malthus was later to defend his own position, notably in *Definitions in Political Economy*, (London: Murray, 1827), pp. 157, 190–202 and *passim*.

[22] *Works*, vol. I, pp. 11 and 63 (cp. also the editor's Introduction, *Works*, vol. I, pp. xxxv, xliv, lxiii). What Ricardo opposes are the doctrines which make the price of commodities depend on the price of labour, such as the 'received doctrines, which maintain that every rise in wages is necessarily transferred to the price of commodities' (ibid., p. 61) on one side *and* the labour commanded measure (ibid., p. 14) on the other. Both aspects – as distinguished above – of Malthus's argument were noticed by Ricardo on reading Malthus's *Principles*, as appears from the correspondence and from his commentaries in the *Notes on Malthus* of 1820. For the first aspect see for example Note 11 (*Works* vol. II, pp. 28–35); the second aspect is first noticed by Ricardo, not without disappointment, in a letter to McCulloch of 2 May 1820 (*Works*, vol. VIII, p. 180), soon after reading Malthus's *Principles*. See also his commentaries, in the *Notes on Malthus*, Notes 24 and 25 (*Works*, vol. II, pp. 62–4). See also below fn. 38.

explains why the present Notes on Malthus's *Measure of Value* were in fact to launch Ricardo once more into 'the interminable controversy about the "measure of value"'.[23] 'I am . . . labouring in my vocation', Ricardo wrote to Malthus, 'and trying to understand the most difficult question in Political Economy'.[24]

As recalled above, the measure of value had been discussed by Malthus in the first edition of his *Principles*. Before the publication of the book, in a letter to Ricardo of 10 September 1819, Malthus had first mentioned the curious example that,

> If we suppose half an ounce of silver on an average to be picked up by a days search on the sea shore, money would then always retain most completely the same value. It would always on an average both cost, and command the same quantity of labour . . . According to my measure of value indeed I should say at once that money had fallen if it would command less labour . . .[25]

The same idea was then taken up and developed in the book, particularly in a section of chapter 2 (on value) which discusses 'the labour which a commodity will command, considered as a measure of real value in exchange'[26] and opens with a reference to Adam Smith describing labour as a measure of value – in the labour-commanded sense – to be 'the best of any one commodity'. Ricardo's criticism of that position, repeated throughout the *Notes* of 1820, was as follows: since Malthus objects to Ricardo's labour-embodied measure of value on the ground that it ignores significant causes of variation, 'would [you] not suppose then that when he proposed a measure of value he would propose one free from these objections?' Surprisingly, '[h]e does quite the contrary, he proposes a measure which is not only variable in itself, but is particularly variable'.[27]

In the pamphlet on the measure of value of 1823, Malthus is again open, in Ricardo's view, to the charge of adopting an 'arbitrary assumption of a measure of value'.[28] It should be noticed, however, that – presumably in response to Ricardo's previous criticisms – Malthus makes an attempt to

23 As expressed in the words of Mrs Grote; see her account of the intellectual atmosphere around Ricardo, in *Works*, vol. IX, pp. 301–2.

24 3 August 1823 (*Works*, vol. IX, p. 325).

25 *Works*, vol. VIII, pp. 64–5; cp. also *Principles*, Pullen edn, vol. I, pp. 110–11.

26 *Principles*, Pullen edn, vol. I, p. 118.

27 Note 38; *Works*, vol. II, pp. 90–1. More precisely, Ricardo's standard of value is, in the first edition of his *Principles*, money (gold) supposed 'to be always the produce of the same quantity of unassisted labour' (*Works*, vol. I, p. 63).

28 Note VIII (below, p. 31). Also, as a further example, Note I (below, pp. 7ff.) and Note II (below, pp. 12ff.), where Ricardo criticizes Malthus for the sudden change of language (p. 10) and for 'an arbitrary selection not founded on any sufficient reason' (p. 14).

justify his own measure on grounds of invariability. The attempt, as we shall see presently, makes him no less liable to Ricardo's charge of arbitrariness. '[I]f it can be shown, that any object', Malthus writes, 'the value of which is composed of two elements, is of such a nature that while the value of one of these elements increases, the value of the other decreases exactly in the same degree, such object must be of a constant value'. Malthus appears to stipulate that such an exact compensation of wages and profits occurs within the constant 'value of the variable quantity of produce which . . . forms the wages of a given number of men'[29]. On that assumption the table which appears on Malthus's page 38 is constructed.[30] What Malthus is really attempting to do is *deduce* that assumption from the observation that the exchangeable value of commodities is 'accurately measured by the quantity of labour which would result from adding to the accumulated and immediate labour actually worked up in them the varying amount of the profits on all the advances estimated in labour', which 'must necessarily be the same as the quantity of labour which they will command'.[31] Ricardo's critical reply is well exemplified by his remark on a passage on Malthus's page 31: 'This is the only passage in which a reason is given for the value of labour being the standard measure of value, and never was there a less logical proof of a proposition advanced.'[32]

The argument is reflected also in the subsequent correspondence between Ricardo and Malthus. 'Is it true then', Ricardo asks, 'that every commodity exchanges for two quantities of labour, one equal to the quantity actually worked up in it, another equal to the quantity which the profits will command?' Can it be true, as a further question, that, since 'profits depend upon the *proportion* of the whole produce which goes to labour, it must necessarily happen that the increase of value [of labour] occasioned by the additional quantity of labour will be exactly counterbalanced by the diminution in the amount of profits, leaving the value of labour the same'?[33] Both questions are answered in the negative by Ricardo and for the same reason: both propositions depend on the arbitrary stipulation that 'labour never varies'. Thus Ricardo's arguments, through the *Notes on Malthus* of

[29] Malthus *Measure of Value*, p. 31, 32; below, pp. 28–9. Cp. Ricardo's Note IX, below, p. 35.

[30] 'Table Illustrating the Invariable Value of Labour and Its Results', below, p. 34.

[31] *Measure of Value*, pp. 15–16; below, p. 17.

[32] Note VI (below, p. 29). For other detailed criticisms on Malthus's Table, see Bailey's *Critical Dissertation*, 1825, ch. 7, pp. 142–51; De Quincey devotes the sixth of his Templars' Dialogues, published in the *London Magazine* for 1824, to a criticism of Malthus's Table.

[33] Letter 536, to Malthus, 3 August 1823, *Works*, vol. IX, pp. 323–4. A further charge of Ricardo against Malthus is not to have consistently employed a measure 'however arbitrarily selected'. See below, Note I, p. 12; cp. e.g. *Notes on Malthus*, Note 63, in *Works*, vol. II, pp. 124–7. Cp. also letter to McCulloch, 2 May 1820, in *Works*, vol. VIII, p. 180.

1820 and the present Notes, are a development of his grounds for opposing Adam Smith on commanded labour as a measure of value. 'The quantity of labour bestowed on any object', Ricardo writes in a well-known passage of the *Principles* and 'the quantity which it can command in the market' cannot be 'two equivalent expressions'. When the latter is taken as a measure of value, the value of an object is made dependent on the value of labour, which is itself variable and thus not a good yardstick. This can only amount, in Ricardo's view, to a *petitio principii*.[34] It should be noted that, in fact, Ricardo's argument provides the rationale in the opening section of his book for the adoption of the labour-embodied theory of value as a means of avoiding circular reasoning.

As was stated above (p. xv), there is a further consequence attached to Malthus's curious example of silver picked up on the sea shore in a day's search. This has to do with the *negative* side of the argument. Malthus's search for a counterexample which would disprove Ricardo's analysis eventually led Ricardo himself to *deny* that a perfect measure of value can be found. A series of reflections on this topic run through Ricardo's writings on value, reaching a final expression during the last stage of his thinking, particularly in the paper on 'Absolute Value and Exchangeable Value'.[35] This line of thought, however, is only hinted at in the present Notes. The 'circumstances' under which commodities are produced are mentioned in Note I and Note II; but – as far as the last stage of Ricardo's thinking is concerned – it is only with Ricardo's letter to Malthus of 28 May 1823 that the issue is faced directly. Ricardo's argument is that Malthus is arbitrarily making *general* use of what only amounts to a *particular* case:

> Your mistake appears to me to be this, you shew us that under certain conditions a certain commodity would be a measure of absolute value, and then you apply it to cases where the conditions are not complied with, and suppose it to be a measure of absolute value in those cases also. You appear to me too to deceive yourself when you think you prove your proposition, because your proof only amounts to this, that your measure is a good measure of exchangeable value, but not of absolute value.

And he concludes:

> My only object has been to shew . . . that a measure of value which is only allowed to be accurate in a particular case where no capital is

[34] *Principles*, chapter 1, section i; *Works*, vol. I, pp. 13–14, 17–19; cp. also above n. 22 fn.

[35] This is the side of the value controversy that has been emphasized by Piero Sraffa; see in part. *Works*, vol. I, pp. xlv–xlvii and vol. IV, pp. 358–9.

employed, is arbitrarily applied by you to cases where capital and time necessarily enter into the consideration.[36]

In later correspondence and in his paper on 'Absolute Value and Exchangeable Value', Malthus's measure is treated, more precisely from Ricardo's own standpoint, as an *extreme* case.[37] '[I]t is in vain', Ricardo writes to McCulloch:

> to attempt to measure value accurately, unless your measure agrees precisely in the proportions of wages and profits with the commodity measured. A commodity which has wages in it alone, and no profits, and this is Malthus's measure, is not an accurate measure for commodities which have both labour and profits in them. All we can do is to make the best choice amongst confessedly imperfect measures, and I should have no hesitation in selecting Malthus's if the number of commodities produced by labour alone were the most numerous . . . I have nothing to amend in the choice I have made; I consider it a mean; Malthus's is at one extreme of the scale, old oak trees are at the other.[38]

What needs to be emphasized is that it is a feature of this line of thought in Ricardo that it is ultimately *negative* in character and eventually leads him to deny that a perfect measure of value can be found.

> You find fault with my measure of value . . . because it varies with the varying profits of other commodities. This is I acknowledge an imperfection in it when used to measure other commodities in which there enters more or less profits than enters into my measure, but you do not appear to see that against your measure the same objection holds good, for your measure contains no profits at all, and therefore never can be an accurate measure of value for commodities which do contain profits.

[36] Letter 529, to Malthus, 28 May 1823; *Works*, vol. IX, pp. 297, 298–9 and 300. In this letter Ricardo is concerned with the *difference*, created by different proportions or durabilities of capital, in the relative value of commodities produced by equal quantities of labour. Cp. the editor's discussion in *Works*, vol. I, pp. xlvii, xlviii.

[37] *Works*, vol. IV, p. 372, and cp. *Works*, vol. I, p. xliv, where this argument of Ricardo's is discussed.

[38] Letter 544, 21 August 1823; *Works*, vol. IX, p. 361. Ricardo was referring here to the defence he had introduced into his *Principles*, 3rd edn, where gold was treated as a commodity produced by means of an average proportion of fixed and circulating capital (see chapter I, sec. vi; *Works*, vol. I, pp. 43–7). This as a line of thought had actually been suggested by Malthus himself in 1820: see *Principles*, Pullen edn, vol. I, pp. 92–4 (cp. *Works*, vol. II, esp. pp. 62–4), where Malthus classified commodities according to the different proportions of fixed and circulating capital employed in their production. Ricardo's reaction to this part of Malthus's *Principles* had marked the appearance of the idea that the search for the invariable standard should lead to an average commodity. See, in particular, Ricardo's Notes 24 and 25 (*Works*, vol. II, pp. 62–4) and cp. *Works*, vol. I, pp. xlii (fn. 4), xliii–xliv.

The conclusion is that 'no accurate measure of absolute value can be found'; 'you claim to have given us an accurate measure of value, and I object to your claim, not that I have succeeded and you have failed, but that we have both failed – that there is not and cannot be an accurate measure of value'.[39] As Ricardo wrote in his last letter to Mill: '[T]here is not in nature any correct measure of value nor can any ingenuity suggest one, for what constitutes a correct measure for some things is a reason why it cannot be a correct one for others.'[40]

The interest attached to the Notes on Malthus's *Measure of Value* is, therefore, that they emphasize Ricardo's criticism of the labour-commanded measure of value for being an *arbitrary* measure, i.e. a variable measure. That invariability is positively required for something to qualify as a proper measure of value remained a fundamental tenet for Ricardo.[41] This particular argument in Ricardo's thought stands out from the opening pages of his *Principles* and runs through the *Notes on Malthus* of 1820 to the present follow-up. It provides the whole basis for Ricardo's adoption and subsequent allegiance to his labour theory of value, which – combined with the principle of diminishing returns – forms the entire foundation of the Ricardian system. It is interesting that it also provides the starting point for the last stage of Ricardo's analysis on value. This parallels a further developing feature of Ricardo's thought, fully highlighted by Sraffa, which describes Malthus's measure of value as an extreme case: the latter originates from chapter 1, section VI of the *Principles*, 3rd edn, and contributes to Ricardo's final disproof of the feasibility of finding a perfect measure of value.

Both arguments are thus prominent in Ricardo's last papers and in the correspondence: the papers, in particular, with the addition of the present Notes, provide a remarkable restatement of the fundamental features of the Ricardian conception of value. In this sense they are part of any accurate reconstruction of what Ricardo believed to be significant in value analysis.

Note and acknowledgements

The present edition reproduces Ricardo's Notes from the *International Review of Economics and Business*, vol. XXVI (1979). The same method is adopted here as in the Sraffa edition of Ricardo's *Notes on Malthus* (*Works*, vol. II, esp. pp. xvi–xviii). The

[39] Letter 542, to Malthus, 15 August 1823, *Works*, vol. IX, pp. 346, 352.
[40] Letter 552 of 5 September 1823; *Works*, vol. IX, p. 387.
[41] This is a point on which Bailey was, a few years later, to concentrate attention, linking Malthus with Ricardo in his attack.

text, spelling and punctuation have been checked against the original MS and the Notes have been numbered progressively, following the order of Malthus's pages to which they refer, by inserting roman numbers at the beginning of each. While in most cases Ricardo gives a reference to the page he is commenting upon, the identification of the relevant passages had to be made through internal evidence, except where a quotation is given by Ricardo himself. Attention is drawn in the footnotes to all corrections of any possible interest, as they appear from the study of the MS. An acknowledgement is due to the editor of the *International Review of Economics and Business* for permission to make use of their edition.

The first publication of Ricardo's *Notes* was encouraged by the late Piero Sraffa, to whom the editor showed a copy of the MS in January 1978. The idea of an edition of the *Notes* as a companion volume to the Royal Economic Society editions of Ricardo and Malthus was first suggested in May 1987 by Roberto Scazzieri. The project could then materialize through the support of Donald Winch, who lent generous help and advice on the editing of the present volume. John Pullen and Roberto Scazzieri also kindly gave their comments on the editorial apparatus. Pier F. Asso and Denis P. O'Brien were helpful on particular points.

'The Measure of Value Stated and Illustrated', with Ricardo's Notes on the text

THE

MEASURE OF VALUE

STATED AND ILLUSTRATED,

WITH

AN APPLICATION OF IT TO THE ALTERATIONS IN THE VALUE OF THE ENGLISH CURRENCY SINCE 1790.

By the Rev. T. R. MALTHUS, M.A. F.R.S.
PROFESSOR OF HISTORY AND POLITICAL ECONOMY IN THE EAST INDIA COLLEGE, HERTFORDSHIRE.

LONDON:
JOHN MURRAY, ALBEMARLE STREET.
MDCCCXXIII.

INTRODUCTION

It may, perhaps, excite some degree of surprize that I should propose, as if it were new, a measure of value, which will be found to be the same as that which has been brought forward by Adam Smith. (iii)

My reasons are the following:–

1st. In laying down labour as a measure of value, it is allowed that he does not make it quite clear, whether he means the labour which is worked up in a commodity, or the labour which it will command; yet they are essentially different.

2dly. In his elaborate inquiry into the value of silver during the four last centuries, he uses corn as his measure, not labour; and arrives at conclusions entirely different from those which would have been the consequence of his using labour. |

3dly. In a case where he specifically states that the money price of labour has risen, he still says, that the value of silver has risen,* which is a direct and express rejection of labour as a measure of value; although he has, in another place, spoken of it as the only universal and accurate measure, and "the only standard by which we can compare the values of different commodities, at all times and at all places."† (iv)

4thly. His reasonings on the subject of the constant value of labour, combined with his application of them, seem rarely to have produced conviction, so that there is no distinguished work on political economy known to me in which labour, in the sense most frequently used by Adam Smith, is

* Book i. c. xi. p. 313, sixth edition.
† Book i. c. v. p. 54, sixth edition.

considered as a standard measure of value, the prevailing opinion being that no such standard is to be found, in which opinion I concurred.‡ |

(v) Under these circumstances, having, by a process quite different from that of Adam Smith, and dependent on doctrines relating to the gradations of soil, which were not noticed by him, arrived at the conclusion, that the labour which commodities will command may be considered as a standard measure of their natural and exchangeable value, I have thought myself justifiable in publishing my view of the subject in its present form. |

‡ Mr. Ricardo has proposed labour as the standard of value, but most expressly rejected the sense in which Adam Smith mainly applies it.

THE MEASURE OF VALUE

It is generally allowed that the word value, in common language, has two different meanings; one, value in use, the other, value in exchange; the first expressing merely the usefulness of an object in supplying the most important wants of mankind, without reference to its power of commanding other objects in exchange; and the second expressing the power of commanding other objects in exchange, without reference to its usefulness in supplying the most important wants of mankind. **[I]** (1)

It is obviously value in the last sense, not the first, with which the science of Political Economy is mainly concerned.

But the power of one object to command another in exchange, or in other words the power of purchasing, may obviously arise either from causes affecting the object itself, or the commodities against which it is exchanged. |

In the one case, the value of the object itself may properly be said to be affected; in the other, only the value of the commodities which it purchases; and if we could suppose any object always to remain of the same value, the (2)

[I][1][2] In this passage as well as in every other where you explain yourself on this subject you make use of the word value to explain what you mean by the word value.

[1] No page reference is given by Ricardo. The first sentence of his comment no doubt refers to Malthus's opening sentence. The remainder of this Note refers to other passages, as indicated by Ricardo.

[2] 'But' is cancelled here.

comparison of other commodities with this one would clearly show, which had risen, which had fallen, and which had remained the same. The value of any commodity estimated in a measure of this kind might with propriety be called its absolute or natural value; while the value of a commodity estimated in others which were liable to variation, whether they were one or many, could only be considered as its nominal or relative value, that is, its value in relation to any particular commodity, or to commodities in general.

That a correct measure of the power of purchasing generally, or of commanding such important commodities as the necessaries and conveniences of life, in whatever way such power might arise, would be very desirable, cannot for a moment be doubted, as it would at once enable us to form a just estimate and comparison of wages, salaries, and revenues, in all countries, and at all periods. But when we consider what such a measure implies, we must feel certain that no one object exists, or can be supposed to
(3) exist, | with such qualities as would fit it to become a standard measure of this kind. It would imply steadiness of value, not merely in one object, but in a great number, which is contrary to all theory and experience.

Whether there is any object, which, though it cannot measure the power of purchasing generally under the varying facilities of production and varying state of the demand and supply by which different commodities are affected, may be a correct measure of absolute and natural value as above described, is the specific object of the present inquiry.

It follows directly, from the principles of Adam Smith, that the conditions of the supply of the great mass of commodities are, that the returns should be sufficient to pay the wages, profits and rents necessary to their production. If these payments be made in money at the ordinary rates of the time, they form what Adam Smith calls their natural prices. Money however we know is variable. But if for money we substitute the objects necessary to give the producer the same power of production and accumulation as the natural money prices would have commanded, such returns

---

At the top of page 4 you speak of natural value without having previously told us what value is. You do indeed immediately after say that natural value are the elements of supply, but surely this is not very clear. Again you say the main elements of value are labour and profits. Page 5. Three hats are now of the same value as a coat – In a month I find 2 hats of the same value Which of them has altered in absolute value? the answer that labour and profits are the

may be considered as the natural conditions of the supply of commodities, and may with pro-|priety be denominated their natural value, in contra- (4)
distinction to their natural price.

Of these three conditions of supply, or elements of natural value, the two first are obviously the most important. They are not only the sole conditions of supply in those early stages of society before the appropriation of land has taken place, but they continue to be so in reference to large classes of objects in the most advanced stages of improvement; and it is now generally acknowledged that even the main vegetable food of an improving country, which is the foundation of wages, must necessarily be of the same value as that part of the produce which is almost exclusively resolvable into wages and profits, and pays very little rent.

We cannot therefore essentially err in assuming for the present that the natural value of objects in their more simple forms is composed of labour and profits,* and the effect of any portion of rent, or of other ingredients which are sometimes added to these elements, may be allowed for subsequently. |

We may also consider as a postulate which will be readily granted, that (5)
any given quantity of labour must be of the same value as the wages which command it, or for which it actually exchanges.

Of the two main elements of value, labour and profits, the former, particularly if we include, as we ought to do, accumulated as well as immediate labour, is much the largest and most powerful.

The great instrument of production is labour. There is no commodity nor implement used to assist manual exertions in which it does not enter as a condition of supply, and very few in which it does not enter very largely. If

* Mr. Ricardo, speaking of the commodities produced by the capitalist, says, "their whole value is divided into two portions only: one constitutes the profits of stock; the other the wages of labour." (p. 107. 3d edit.) The language of Mr. Mill, in his *Elements of Political Economy*, is similar.

---

elements[3] of value does not satisfy the question, because under all[4] circumstances the hats and the coat are[5] composed of these elements. What I want specifically to know is why I am to compare them to labour to ascertain that fact, rather than to gold, corn, or any other thing, and on this point you give me no satisfactory answer.

[3] The following words are interlined from this point: 'and therefore the quantity of labour necessary to produce the labour and profits together'.

[4] 'the' is cancelled here.

[5] The following words are interlined from this point: 'and therefore I must'.

in the production of commodities and of the implements which assist in this production, no other ingredient were required than labour, and the interval between the exertion of the labour and its remuneration in the completed commodity were so inconsiderable that it might be entirely disregarded, it is certain that, as the same quantity of labour would have a constant tendency to produce commodities in the same relative proportion to each other, and to the demand for them, they would be found on an average to
(6) exchange with each other according to the | quantity of labour which had been employed to obtain them.

Thus if ten mackerel were, on an average, obtained by the same quantity of labour as two soals, it would be necessary, in order to continue the supply of both in the market, that the value of a soal should be five times as great in the power of purchasing similar commodities, as the value of a mackerel; because if it were less, none would apply themselves to the catching of soals; and though it is quite certain that at any given period the relative value of soals and mackerel would be exclusively determined by the state of the demand and supply of each; and that they would, in consequence, often vary very considerably; yet it is as certain, that on the supposition of the hypothesis being correct, and that they both continued to be brought to market, each would on an average be supplied in such a quantity, compared

---

What do you say in page 7? « With regard(6) the same . . . and any given quantity of labour [»]. But(7) fish will(8) feed the workman. Now(9) suppose that notwithstanding the cheapness of soals and mackerel labour was so plentiful that no more of these commodities were given for a day's labour than before, altho 50 pc. more of them were given for every other commodity would it be right for you immediately to change your language and say(10) mackerel and soals had not altered in value but every other commodity had. When labour may be increased and diminished – when it may from one year(11) to another be rendered abundant or scarce why should we

6 Last two words replace 'And if'.
7 'as' is cancelled here.
8 The words 'had become cheaper' are written above the last three words, which are however not cancelled.
9 Inserted.
10 The remainder of this Note is written on a letter cover, on which a postmark with the date of 7 April 1823 is discernible.
11 Replaces 'day'.

with the demand for it, that a soal would ordinarily exchange for five mackerel, and the different quantities of labour required to produce them would, in this case, be a correct measure both of their natural and relative value in exchange.

Now supposing that the skill and power of the labourers were so to increase, that, in the | same time and with the same personal exertions, they (7)
could obtain three soals and fifteen mackerel, it is obvious that the relative value of soals to mackerel would remain the same, but they would both have essentially altered their value compared with all those commodities which still required the same quantity of labour to produce the same supply of them. With regard to such commodities, soals and mackerel would have become of less value, and consequently they would have become of less value with regard to a given quantity of labour. The correct language in this case would be, not that labour had become dearer, but that soals and mackerel had become cheaper. And if the same increase of skill and power could be conceived to extend to all other commodities, and all commodities were similarly circumstanced as to their mode of production and bringing to market; it cannot be doubted, that though they might retain the same relative value compared with each other, they would all become more plentiful with regard to the wants of the society, and any given quantity of

---

assume that it is invariable?[(12)] On this I rest our controversy, the correct language that which mankind universally use is to say that labour, and fish have fallen in value and all other things have continued unaltered[(13)]. You indeed assume in your argument that fish is the immediate produce of unassisted labour which is far from being the fact – the fisherman requires nets, and a boat the profits on which fixed capital cannot fail to affect the value of fish.

We fully allow that the deer and canoe under the circumstances you suppose would vary as you say but we ask[(14)] why the variations should be measured in the standard you propose rather than in any other.

[12] The following sentence is cancelled here: 'The correct language would be as you say if more fish [were given] for given labour that all'. The words in brackets are inserted.

[13] 'You require' and 'You must not answer me by saying that' are deleted at this point.

[14] 'if they will not' is cancelled here. On the comparison of deer and canoe, see Malthus's pp. 9–10 (below, p. 14).

labour. And the correct language would still be, not that labour had become dearer, but that all commodities had become cheaper. **[II]** This fall would
(8) be a fall in the absolute and natural value of commodities; | and as long as labour alone was concerned in their production, and they were brought to market immediately, it would be allowed that the different quantities of labour employed upon them would be a correct measure both of their relative value compared with each other, and of their absolute and natural value in reference to the conditions of their supply. Their natural values would be exactly represented by the different quantities of labour worked up in them; while their natural prices would be these different quantities of labour estimated in money, according to the money price of the labour employed.

But at a very early period of society a considerable interval must elapse between the exertion of some sorts of labour and the completion of the article on which they are employed. And the next simplest form of production, beyond the result of mere labour, is that, where, in addition to the labour employed directly on the commodity and on the simple tools necessary to its production, the condition of the supply requires that a

---

In chusing labour as your measure of value you must of course contend that labour is invariable. Suppose half the people carried off by an epidemic disease the reward of labour would be exceedingly high and every body would say that labour was dear – you however would tell us that we were quite mistaken and that commodities were exceedingly cheap. I believe such cheapness would not be very desirable to the mass of consumers.

I do not say that you may not nor that you have not argued consistently from your measure of value – all the phenomena of political economy may be explained(15) with any measure however arbitrarily selected – I think you have arbitrarily selected yours and by so doing have made the science more difficult. It is quite possible according to your(16)

[II] Page 6 and 7 – Mr. M allows the whole for which I contend(1)

15 'however' is cancelled here.

16 The sentence breaks off at this point. For a similar statement, cp. Ricardo's letter to Malthus of 29 April 1823 (*Works*, vol. IX, p. 281). On the epidemic disease, cp. *ibid.* p. 282 and below, Note VIII, p. 31.

1 'and' is cancelled here.

certain compensation be made in the final remuneration for the time which has elapsed from the period of the advances of the labour, to the period when the labourer, or capitalist, can be remunerated. This compensa-|tion, (9)
which equally applies to the formation of the capital, as to the products to be obtained by it, is the profit which must be paid on the advances of the labour, and is absolutely necessary to the encouragement of such advances.

But in this state of things commodities would cease to exchange with each other according to the quantity of labour employed upon them. Some commodities, on which the same quantity of accumulated and immediate labour had been employed, would be of a different exchangeable value, on account of the different quantity of profits which had entered into their composition; while others, on which different quantities of accumulated and immediate labour had been employed, might be of the same exchangeable value, on account of the greater quantity of profits of which they were composed being balanced by the smaller quantity of labour advanced to produce them.

---

he admits that if all commodities were produced under the same circumstances then their value would be regulated by the quantity of labour actually employed upon them.

Suppose the fact to be so for a moment, would not Mr. M then allow that if with the labour of 10 men 300 qrs. of corn were produced at one time, and 150 only[(2)] at another corn would fall 50 pc. and exchange for one half[(3)] less quantity of cloth shoes etc. in which no alteration[(4)] with respect to facility of production had taken place? He must allow this by his own concession in page 7 where he speaks of soals and mackerel, for he there says « With regard to such commodities . . . quantity of labour »

In this supposition it is true Mr. M imagines that a given quantity of fish as well as of every thing else[(5)] would exchange for only half the former quantity of labour which it could command and as labour is his measure of value he might say the commodities were all cheaper, but would they not be equally cheap and abundant if notwithstanding the facility of their production they, in consequence

[2] Inserted. [3] 'one half' replaces 'a'. [4] 'had' is cancelled here.

[5] Written first 'that fish as well as every thing else', then modified to the reading of the text.

In the earliest stages of society accumulations of capital are very rare, and profits may be extremely high, perhaps forty or fifty per cent. If under these circumstances the construction of a war canoe were to take two years before it were fit for use, it is evident that its value in exchange would be
(10) prodigiously enhanced by such profits. Compared with a | number of deer which might have cost exactly the same quantity of accumulated and immediate labour to bring to market, the canoe would be seventy or eighty per cent. of greater value; and on the fall of profits from forty or fifty per cent. to ten per cent. in the progress of society, an object of this kind might fall in value sixty or seventy per cent. compared with such objects as deer or fish, without any difference in the quantity of labour employed upon either.

It is observed by Adam Smith that corn is an annual crop, butchers' meat a crop which requires four or five years to grow; and consequently, if we compare two quantities of corn and beef which are of equal exchangeable value, it is certain that a difference of three or four additional years profit at fifteen per cent. upon the capital employed in the production of the beef would, exclusively of any other considerations, make up in value for a much smaller quantity of labour, and thus we might have two commodities of the same exchangeable value, while the accumulated and immediate labour of the one was forty or fifty per cent. less than that of the other. This is an event of daily occurrence in reference to a vast mass of the most important commodities in the country; and if profits were to fall from fifteen per
(11) cent. | to eight per cent. the value of beef compared with corn would fall above twenty per cent.

When commodities are obtained by the assistance of a large proportion of fixed capital of a very durable nature, the advances are only consumed in part, and the whole produce of the accumulated and immediate labour employed must be considered as composed of the new produce obtained, together with the remainder of the fixed capital which is unconsumed.* In reference to the separate value of the new produce, this will be the same as if

* This is very properly stated by Colonel Torrens, in his *Production of Wealth*, c. 1. p.28.

---

of the increase of population and the supply of labour exchanged for precisely the same quantity of labour as before. Mr. M may say no and may argue as I think he does on the measure of value which he has chosen but it is nevertheless an arbitrary selection not founded on any sufficient reason and therefore unsatisfactory as a scientific measure.

to the labour actually worked up in such produce were added the profits of the whole capital advanced. It sometimes happens that the proportion of value arising from these profits is very considerable; and commodities so produced will necessarily have much less labour worked up in them, and will be much more affected in their value by a rise or fall of profits, than those which are composed mainly of immediate labour.

Thus, if a commodity were produced by the aid of accumulated labour in machinery worth £2,000, the annual wear and tear of which was | one-twentieth, or £100, and the labour employed on cheap materials and in (12) the working of the machinery were worth £200, while profits were 20 per cent. then the value of the labour worked up in the commodity would be £100 added to £200, equal to £300; and the whole capital advanced being £2,300, the profits upon it would be £460, which, added to £300 would make the whole value of the produce £760. Compared with a commodity of equal value which had been produced without fixed capital, and had yet been brought to market in the same time and with the same rate of profits, it would contain less than half of the labour worked up in it; while, if profits were to fall from 20 per cent. to 10 per cent. the value of the commodity would fall in the proportion of from £760 to £530, or, if profits had been 10 per cent. and were to rise to 20 per cent. the value of the commodity would rise in the proportion of from £530 to £760, or above 42 per cent., without any change in the quantity of labour employed.* |

(13) It must be allowed, then, that whenever two elements are necessary to the supply, and enter into the composition of commodities, their value cannot depend exclusively upon one of them, except by accident, or when the other

* The effects of slow or quick returns, and of the different proportions of fixed and circulating capitals, are distinctly allowed by Mr. Ricardo; but in his last edition, (the third, p. 32.) he has much underrated their amount. They are both theoretically and practically so considerable as entirely to destroy the position that commodities exchange with each other according to | the quantity of labour which has been employed upon them; but no one that I am aware of has ever stated that the different quantity of labour employed on commodities is not a much more powerful source of difference of value.

In a bad harvest the labourer would get with the same money wages a less quantity of corn – if he got before 10 qrs. he might then only get 8 and consequently the real value of corn according to Mr. Malthus would rise one fourth, that is to say would rise exactly in proportion to the diminished quantity given to the labourer. But it has been the object of Mr. Tooke's book to shew that the effect on

can be considered as a given or common quantity. But it is universally acknowledged, that the great mass of commodities in civilized and improved countries is made up at the least of two elements – labour and profits; consequently, the exchangeable value of commodities into which these two elements enter as the conditions of their supply, will not depend exclusively upon the quantity of labour employed upon them, except in the very peculiar cases when both the returns of the advances and the proportions of fixed and circulating capitals are exactly the same.

It cannot, then, be said with any thing like an approximation towards correctness, that the labour worked up in commodities is the measure of their exchangeable value.

(14) But if to the accumulated and immediate la-|bour worked up in commodities, we add the profits upon the whole advances for the time that they are advanced, we shall then make the proper allowance for the other element of value, and may expect to obtain a more accurate measure. If we had estimated the value of the labour advanced in money, or any other medium, we should of course estimate the profits in the same medium, and the natural price of the commodity estimated in such medium, would obviously be equal to the price of the accumulated and immediate labour expended on the commodity, together with the ordinary profits estimated upon such advances. But if, with a view to the natural conditions of supply, we consider only the quantity of labour advanced, without reference to any other medium, we must of course estimate the profits in quantity of labour also, which will give us an amount of labour in proportion to which commodities will be found to exchange with each other, just in the same way as they would exchange with each other according to the quantity of

---

value of a diminished quantity is much greater than in this proportion.[(6)] It by no means follows because the labourer is reduced to ¾ of his former allowance that therefore the landlord and farmer have each to put up with an equal reduction – the contrary I believe to be the fact therefore[(7)]

[6] Thomas Tooke *Thoughts and Details on the High and Low Prices of the Last Thirty Years. Part I, On the Alterations in the Currency*, London: Murray, 1823. Cp. *Works*, vol. IX, p. 250; also below, Malthus's pp. 66 and fn. 70; Malthus reviewed Tooke's work in the *Quarterly Review*, vol. XXIX, April 1823, art. VIII, p. 214; cp. *Principles*, Pullen edn, Introduction to vol. I, p. xlvii.

[7] The Note breaks off at this point.

labour employed on them, if labour had been the sole ingredient which had entered into their composition.

Thus, if a hundred days labour were employed upon a commodity, at two shillings a day, and | the average interval between the advance of such (15) wages and the period when the commodity could be brought to sale were a year, and profits were 20 per cent. the price of the commodity would be £12, while the price of a commodity which had cost the same quantity of labour of the same kind, and could be brought to market immediately, would be only £10. And it is equally certain, that, if putting money or any other medium of exchange out of the question, we had estimated the profits for a year upon the advances of the hundred days labour actually employed, we should obtain a quantity of labour which, compared with the labour employed on the commodity sold immediately, would be in the proportion of 120 to 100, and expressing the relative conditions of supply, would accurately measure the rate at which the two commodities obtained under these different circumstances would exchange with each other.

It appears, then, that in the same country, and at the same time, the exchangeable value of those commodities which can be resolved into labour and profits alone, would be accurately measured by the quantity of labour which would result from adding to the accumulated and immediate labour actually worked up in them the varying amount of the profits on all | the (16) advances estimated in labour.**[III]** But this must necessarily be the same as the quantity of labour which they will command, as appears from the instances above stated, and will be more fully shown farther on; and where the precious metals may be considered for short periods as of a uniform value, the conformity of this measure with the proportions of money prices

---

[III] [Page 15. Cloth can be resolved into labour and profits alone, but it will not be accurately measured by this rule. Suppose 110 of any commodity to be the produce of[(1)] the labour of 50 men for a year, and the profits of stock to be 10 pc, the commodity will be of the value of 55 mens labour for a year and 100 will be paid to labourers and 10 to profits[(2)]. Suppose profits to fall one half the cloth ought according to this rule to be worth the value of 52½ mens labour for a year[(3)] and as labour is worth 20 times the profits the

[1] Last nine words replace '100 pieces of cloth to be worth'.
[2] The last eleven words, following the word 'year', are inserted.
[3] The words that follow, to complete the sentence, are interlined from this point.

at which commodities would be exchanging all around us, might daily be brought to the test of experience and be established beyond the possibility of doubt.

It will be said, perhaps, that in the same place, and at the same time, almost every commodity may be considered as an accurate measure of the relative value of others, and that what is true of labour in this respect is true of cloth, cotton, iron, or any other article. Any two commodities which, at the same time, and in the same place, will purchase or command the same quantity of cloth, cotton, or iron, of a given quality, will have the same relative value, or will exchange with each other.

This will be readily granted, if we take the same time and place exactly, and consider only relative value; but not if either any latitude be allowed as to time and place, or if we consider, as it is our object to do, not merely
(17) relative, but | absolute and natural value. Cloth, cotton, iron, and similar commodities, are subject to vary most essentially in a single year, or even month, so that the manufacturer who could obtain for his goods the same quantity of cloth as he could the year before, would be very little likely to obtain the same quantity of other articles. But even supposing that these articles and the product of the capitalist were to continue of the same relative value to each other, he might still be quite unable to carry on his business. The conditions of the supply of commodities do not require that they should retain always the same relative values, but that each should retain its proper *natural* value, or the means of obtaining those objects which will continue to the producer the same power of production and accumulation. If the advances of capitalists consisted specifically in cloth, then these advances would always have the effect required in production; and as profits are calculated upon the advances necessary to production, whatever they may be, the quantity of cloth advanced, with the addition of the ordinary profits estimated also in quantity of cloth, would represent both the natural

---

labourers will receive[4] 104.76 and profits 5.23. But this will not be true[5] for if 110 be worth 52½ : : 104.76–[6]: 50 and 5.23 : 2½][7]

4 '5.23' is cancelled here.

5 The following passage is deleted at this point: 'in Mr. M's measure. For suppose labour to rise 10 pc. the ['advances will increase from 50 to 55 and 100 will command' was deleted in the process of writing the passage] 110 pieces of cloth will then only command 52^{38} [first written '50', then corrected to 52^{38}] days labour, and the advances will be increased from'.

6 Replaces '95.2'.

7 This whole Note, inserted in square brackets, is cancelled.

and relative value of the commodity. But the specific advances of capitalists do not consist of cloth, but of labour;**[IV]** | and as no other object what- (18)
ever can represent a given quantity of labour, it is obvious that labour stands quite alone in this respect, and that it is the quantity of *labour* which a

---

[IV] 17. The condition of supply of a particular commodity is that it should be sufficiently valuable to afford a profit after paying the labour necessary to its production. This is the same thing as to say that the whole of the commodity when produced must not be given to the(1) labourers only, but must be divided amongst labourers and capitalists.

Because labour is necessary to production a thing is valuable according to the quantity of labour it can command. Why? According to this system if you were to double the quantity of capital(2) in the country it would be of double the value if you could command twice the quantity of labour with it, but it would be no more valuable if wages were increased in the same proportion(3)

[If 2/– in silver could be picked up in a day 2/– would be always of the same value as a day's labour If a certain quantity(4) of corn could be produced in a year by the labour of 100 men and if profits were 10 pc.(5) its value would be 110(6) times 2/– it would command the labour of 110 men. Now suppose profits to(7) remain the same and that double the quantity of produce be obtained with the same labour it is obvious that corn would fall to half its former price. Would this be so? It would be divided in the following proportions 80.20. – but 91 to 80 is not as 125 to 110](8).

1 Inserted. 2 'and of annual fund' was first inserted here and then deleted.

3 This objection finds an analogous expression in Ricardo's letter to Malthus of 13 July 1823. See *Works*, vol. IX, p. 305.

4 First written 'If 100 bushels' then corrected to 'If 10 bushels', finally modified as in the text.

5 Last six words are inserted. 6 Replaces '100'.

7 The following words are interlined from this point, without any part of the sentence in the text being cancelled: 'rise to 25 pc. and the same quantity of corn to be produced the value ought to be 125 times 2/–'. The last two sentences of this Note evidently take this supposition into account.

8 This whole paragraph, as bracketed, is deleted. A few figures appear at this point in the MS, no doubt connected with the arithmetic operations Ricardo was performing for his numerical example.

commodity will command, and not the quantity of any other commodity, which can represent the conditions of its supply, or its natural value.* **[V]**

It will be allowed, then,

First, that when commodities are obtained by labour alone, and sold immediately, they will, on an average, exchange with each other according to the quantity of labour employed upon them.

Secondly, that when profits are concerned, and differ either in rate or quantity, commodities can no longer exchange with each other, according to the quantity of labour employed upon them, except by accident.

Thirdly, that the quantity of accumulated and immediate labour applied
(19) to their production, must, in all the less complex cases, form | the advances on which profits may be correctly calculated.

And, fourthly, that when profits are calculated upon these advances, a quantity of labour is obtained, according to which it is found, by experience, that commodities do exchange with each other in the same country; and, further, that this quantity of labour not only expresses correctly their value in exchange with each other, but their absolute and natural value in reference to the conditions of their supply.

In proceeding to consider what takes place in different countries where the value of the precious metals is very different, it will readily be acknowledged, that the rate at which commodities exchange with each other is not proportioned to the labour which has been employed upon

* Colonel Torrens, by representing capital under the form of certain quantities of cloth and corn, instead of value in labour, has precluded himself from the possibility of giving a just view either of value, profits, or effectual demand. An increase of cloth and corn from the same quantity of labour is of no avail whatever in increasing value, profits, or effectual demand, if this increased produce will not command so much labour as before, an event which is continually occurring, from deficiency of demand.

[V] 18. This is not true. If profits be 10 pc. it is necessary that the commodity produced be equal to the value of the advances with an(1) increased value of 10 pc. If the advances be estimated by the quantity of labour which they will command the produce must command 10 pc. more, – but if the advances be estimated in Iron, Sugar, Coffee, or(2) money is not the same thing true? Why then claim for labour a distinction to which it is by no means entitled

Two countries are equally(3) skilful and industrious but in one the

[1] Last two words are inserted. [2] Inserted.
[3] 'populous and' is cancelled here.

them, with the addition of profits. And it is quite certain, that they cannot be proportioned to the quantity of labour alone of which they are composed. We know, from experience, that the commodities of different countries are actually exchanged with each other according to their money prices at the time. These prices must be determined partly by those natural elements of value which determine the rate at which commodities ex-| change with each other, and the natural conditions of their supply in each (20)
country, and partly by the different value of the precious metals in different situations, which must necessarily have a most powerful effect on the rate at which foreign commodities are exchanged.

Knowing then the elements of the natural and relative value of commodities in the same country, if we knew also the difference in the value of money in different countries, we should know at once the rate at which the commodities of different countries would exchange with each other.

Now there is no supposition but one, relating to the value of money in different countries, which, combined with the natural elements of the value of produce in each, would constitute the present natural prices of commodities in these countries, or the rates at which they actually exchange with each other. This is the supposition that the differences in the value of money in different countries are proportioned to the differences in the money prices of agricultural labour.* |

* Agricultural labour is taken for the obvious reasons that it is the commonest species of labour, that it directly produces the food of the labourer, and that it is the most immediately con-|nected with the gradations of soil, and the necessary variations of profits. It is also assumed with Adam Smith, Mr. Ricardo, and other political economists, that, on an average, other kinds of labour continue to bear the same proportions to agricultural labour.

---

people live on potatoes in the other they live on the best wheat. It will be allowed by Mr. M that in the one country profits will be very high and that in the other they will be comparatively low. He will allow too that there may be as many commodities relatively dear in money price(4) in the one country as in the other and therefore there may be an active commerce between them. A commodity however of the value of £100 will command 2 or 3 times the quantity of labour in the one country that it will command in the other, and therefore Mr. Malthus is bound to say it is 2 or 3 times more

4 'in money price' replaces 'and cheap'.

(21) The conditions of the supply of an Indian commodity are the advance and consumption of a certain quantity of Indian labour, with the profits on all the advances for the time that they are employed. Thus, if for the production of an Indian commodity, a fixed capital consisting of accumulated labour and profits, equal to 300 days, were advanced for a year, and a quantity of accumulated and immediate labour, consisting of the wear and tear of the machinery, the materials to be worked up, and direct labour, equal to 1500 days, were consumed on the commodity in the same time, profits being 20 per cent., the natural value of such commodity in India would be equal to the 1500 days labour consumed, with a profit of 20 per cent. upon 1800 days labour, which would amount to 1860 days labour.

If labour in India were fourpence a day, the fixed money capital in this case would equal £5, the labour advanced and consumed £25, and the labour consumed, together with the profits on the whole advances, would
(22) be equal to £31. | And this would evidently be the natural price at which the commodity would circulate, and according to which it would exchange with any foreign commodity brought to India.

On the same principle, if for the production of an English commodity, 300 days labour were advanced in fixed capital for a year, and 1500 days labour were consumed on the commodity in the same time, while profits were 10 per cent., the natural value of such commodity, or the conditions of its supply, would be 1500 days labour, with a profit of 10 per cent. upon 1800, which together would equal 1680; and if labour were two shillings a day, the natural price at which the commodity would circulate, and according to which it would exchange with any foreign commodity brought to England, would be £168. This prodigious difference in the natural prices of two commodities in England and India, the natural values of which in each country were nearly the same, could only arise from a difference in the value of money occasioned by the very superior efficiency of English labour in the purchase of the precious metals, owing to the

---

valuable.(5) He would however(6) contend that money was of very different values in the two countries, because money as well as other things would command more labour in one country than in the other. Here then we should have all things in the 2 countries of nearly the same money value(7), of nearly the same relative values and yet because they differed only in their power of commanding labour

5 'I suspect however that' is cancelled here.
6 Inserted. 7 Inserted.

energy, skill, and situation of English labourers and capitalists, compared with those of India. But in estimating this difference in the value of money in England and | India, it is quite obvious, that if, after ascertaining the (23)
natural conditions of the supply of a commodity in each country, we were to estimate the value of money either by its general power of purchasing, by a mean between corn and labour,* or by the quantity of labour alone which had been actually employed in bringing the money from the mine to the market, or by any other measure whatever, except the labour which it would command, we should not account for the natural prices which are found actually to prevail in the two countries, and according to which Indian and English commodities are found to exchange with each other by experience.

Consequently, as no other supposition will suit the actual phenomena, and as it has already appeared that the value of commodities in the same country is determined by the quantity of labour which they will command, we may safely conclude that the value of the precious metals in different countries is determined by the same measure, or by the different quantities of common agricultural labour, taking the ave-|rage of summer and winter (24)
wages, which a given portion of them will command.

When we come to consider the varying value of commodities at distant periods in the same country, or the rise or fall of produce in the progress of cultivation and improvement, we are necessarily deprived of the test of an actual exchange. We know, however, that at different periods in the same country both the value of the precious metals, and the rate of profits and corn wages, may alter most essentially.

The effect of the varying value of the precious metals, when we have once obtained a measure of value, will be easily estimated. The most

* In my last work, I thought that a mean between corn and labour might be a better measure of value than labour alone; but I am now convinced that I was wrong, and that labour alone is the true measure.

Mr. Malthus would say they were all 2 or 3 times dearer in one than in the other. Would not all mankind agree in this case that the right way of describing the state of things in these 2 countries would be to say that commodities were nearly of the same value in each but that labour was twice or thrice as cheap in one as in the other[(8)]

[8] See the argument developed in Malthus's pp. 20–4. This paragraph appears to have been inserted, with alterations, by Ricardo in his letter to Malthus of 29 April 1823. See *Works*, vol. IX, pp. 282–3.

important point at present is, to consider the effects which must be produced upon the value of commodities in the progress of society, by the changes which necessarily take place in the profits of stock and the corn wages of labour.

On the supposition of high profits at an early period of society, and a considerable fall of them subsequently, how are we to measure and compare the value of commodities at these different periods? With regard to those which had continued to cost the same quantity of accumulated and immediate labour, we could not say that they were of the same value,
(25) un-|less we were prepared to assert that the value of commodities is determined solely by the labour employed upon them, not only when the rate of profits is the same but when it is totally different;* a proposition which no one can venture to assert in the case of foreign commodities, and which there is as little reason to assert in comparing the commodities of distant periods.

If profits were 50 per cent. five hundred years ago, and are 10 per cent. now, the question is, whether a piece of cloth which had cost the same quantity of labour at these different periods would be of the same value. By the supposition it was composed of a greater quantity of profits in the earlier period, and having cost the same quantity of labour, we should naturally conclude that it would be of a higher value.

It is said, however, that, although it cost the same quantity of labour, yet
(26) that the labour in the former period was of much less value, | which would counterbalance the greater quantity of profits, and leave the value obtained by the same quantity of labour the same. But when we are thus referred to the lower value of labour, the principle of compensation which had before been applied is quite forgotten. The corn which pays the labourer is indeed

* Whenever it is said that the value of labour rises in the progress of cultivation, a comparison is made between the value of a given quantity of labour at two different periods; and when it is added that wages rise in proportion to the quantity of labour required to produce them, objects are measured solely by the quantity of labour employed upon them, although the rate of profits may be totally different.

If wages are invariable, the value of corn, must, on your system, be invariable whether the land be fertile and will give 150 qrs. to the labour of 10 men, or comparatively barren and only give 80 qrs. But during the period from the productiveness of labour on the land to its comparative unproductiveness we may suppose no change in the productiveness of labour in manufactures yet they will fall prodigiously in your measure of value, and why? that you have not told

obtained by a smaller quantity of labour, on account of the superior fertility of the soil from which it is raised, but it is sold as the cloth is sold, at a profit of 50 per cent.; and if it be said that, in the case of the cloth, the low value of wages which is supposed to be the result of superior fertility counteracts the high profits and keeps the value of cloth the same, surely it may be said, in the case of the corn which pays the wages, that the smaller quantity of labour necessary to produce it is made up by the greater rate of profits at which it is sold, and the value of wages is thus kept the same.

If 100 quarters of corn be obtained in the different periods of society by the labour of a different number of men, such as 7, 8 and 9, each paid at the rate of 10 quarters a year, the value of the 100 quarters of corn, or the value of the wages of any one of the men employed, estimated in the labour
advanced, with the | addition of the profits upon such advances, must (27)
obviously always be the same.

At an early period of society, when the soil was very fertile and the labour of 7 men only was necessary to produce 100 quarters of corn on land which paid little or no rent, the advances in labour being 7 men, or in corn 70 quarters, and the return 100 quarters, the rate of profits would be $42\frac{6}{7}$ per cent., and the advances of the labour of 7 men increased by a profit of $42\frac{6}{7}$ would equal the labour of 10 men, or the quantity of labour which the whole return would command. At a more advanced period, when the last land taken into cultivation was less fertile, and the labour of 8 men was necessary to obtain the return of 100 quarters, the advances in labour being 8 men, or in corn 80 quarters, the rate of profits would be 25 per cent., and the labour of 8 men increased by 25 per cent. would exactly equal the labour of 10 men. On the same principle, if at a still later period 9 men were necessary to produce the 100 quarters, the rate of profits would be $11\frac{1}{9}$ per cent., and the quantity of labour employed increased by the profits would still be equal to the labour of 10 men.

It appears then that when the labourer con-|tinues to be paid the same (28)

---

us. Why should not the value of the[9] quantity of labour required to produce the wages of ten men when paid in cloth together with the value of the quantity retained for profits on the advances of labour, be as invariable as the same items when employed on the land. Do you not select without giving a sufficient reason one measure rather than another? I ask, why does cloth fall in value in your measure?

9 'value of the' replaces 'produce'.

corn wages, the value of the whole corn produce, or the value of each man's wages estimated in the usual way in labour and profits, must obviously remain constant, and that it must be most erroneous to infer that labour rises in value because it requires more labour in the progress of cultivation to produce the wages of 10 men or one man, if at the same time it requires such a diminished value of profits as exactly to balance it.

But in the progress of cultivation, the corn wages of labour do not continue the same, and corn must consequently be liable to great variation of value, both on account of temporary variations in the state of the supply compared with labour, and on account of the more permanent state of the demand and supply of corn compared with labour, owing to the increasing difficulty of production.

It may be laid down, however, as a general proposition, liable to no exception, that when the value of any produce can be resolved into labour and profits, then as the *proportion* of such produce which goes to labour increases, the proportion which goes to profits must decrease in the same
(29) degree, and as the *proportion* which | goes to labour decreases, the proportion which goes to profits must increase in the same degree.*

* This proposition is essentially the same as that which is very clearly and ably expressed by Mr. Ricardo in his chapter on Profits, (p. 128. 3d ed.) in the following terms: "in all countries and at all times profits depend on the quantity of labour requisite to provide necessaries for the labourers on that land, or with that capital which yields no rent;" a proposition which though incomplete in reference to the ultimate causes of the variations of profits, contains a most important truth. From this truth the legitimate deduction appears to me to be, the constant value of labour; but Mr. Ricardo has formed his system on a deduction exactly opposite to it. He has, however, in my opinion, amply compensated for the errors into which he may have fallen, by furnishing us, at the same time, not only with the means of their refutation, but the means of improving the science of Political Economy.

You tell me it does, but you do not tell me why, and without telling me why when nothing has occurred to alter the circumstances under which cloth is produced I can come to no other conclusion that you have made an arbitrary selection of one commodity as a measure of value which you have only the same right to do as any other man has to select another. One might chuse cloth and another shoes, and they would be as much justified in doing so as you are in chusing labour or corn for in fact they are from particular circumstances nearly the same.[10]

[10] Cloth falling in value is discussed in Malthus's p. 25, above, p. 24.

Thus if $\frac{3}{4}$ of the produce, whatever that produce may be, go to labour, $\frac{1}{4}$ will remain for profits; if $\frac{5}{6}$ go to labour, $\frac{1}{6}$ will remain for profits; and if $\frac{1}{2}$ only go to labour, $\frac{1}{2}$ will remain for profits.

In reference to corn or commodities in general, compared with each other at different periods in the progress of cultivation, it is obvious that neither an increase in the quantity of labour required to produce them, nor an increase in the quantity of produce awarded to the labourer, can ever determine the proportion | of the whole produce which goes to labour and (30) affect profits accordingly; because if the quantity of labour required to produce them increases, the effect of this upon profits may be totally destroyed by a diminution at the same time of the quantity of produce awarded to the labourer; or if a larger quantity of produce be awarded to the labourer, it may be only in consequence of a smaller quantity of labour being necessary to obtain the same produce, in which case profits may remain undiminished, or even rise, at the same time that corn wages rise.

But if instead of referring to commodities generally, we refer to the variable quantity of produce which, under different circumstances, forms the wages of a given number of labourers, we shall find that the variable quantity of labour required to obtain this produce will always exactly agree with the proportion of the whole produce which goes to labour; because, however variable may be the amount of this produce, it will be divided into a number of parts equal to the number of labourers which it will command,

---

Suppose when 150 qrs. of corn are produced by the labour of 10 men and the yearly wages to each man is 10 qrs.[11] 150 pieces of cloth are produced with the same capital and labour and the yearly wages of each man is 10 pieces profits will as you correctly shew in your table 50 pc. Suppose now the last land to be less fertile and that ten men produce only 110 qrs. receiving as before 10 qrs. each profits by your[12] table[13] would be reduced to .91 pc. but the value of 100 qrs. of corn would be in your standard measure the same as before. At this time I will suppose labour to be equally productive in the manufacture of cloth, but as profits are reduced to .91 pc. in this line as well as in every other of the 150 pieces produced the master will have only 13.6 pieces while the labourers will have 136.4 pieces. While no greater quantity of corn was given to the labourers, a much

[11] 'profits' is cancelled here.
[12] MS reads 'yours'.
[13] See Note IX, below, p. 35.

and as the first set of labourers who produced these wages may be considered as having been paid at the same rate as the second set, whose
(31) labour the pro-duce commands; it is obvious that if to obtain the pro-|duce which commands ten labourers, 6, 7, 8, or 9 labourers be required, the proportion of the produce which goes to labour, in these different cases, will be $\frac{6}{10}$, $\frac{7}{10}$, $\frac{8}{10}$, or $\frac{9}{10}$, leaving $\frac{4}{10}$, $\frac{3}{10}$, $\frac{2}{10}$, or $\frac{1}{10}$, for profits.

It is impossible to refer what is proposed as a standard to any *other* measure, because, in that case, the other measure would be the standard. But if it can be shown, that any object, the value of which is composed of two elements, is of such a nature that while the value of one of these elements increases, the value of the other decreases exactly in the same degree, such object must be of a constant value. If the values of two variable quantities, *X* and *Y*, be equal to the constant value *A*, it follows that, in all the variations to which *X* and *Y* are subject, whatever value *X* gains must be lost by *Y*, and whatever value *Y* gains must be lost by *X*.**[VI]** The converse of this proposition must also be true, that is, if the value of any object be made up of the variable values of two other objects, and it can be shown that, from the nature of these two objects, whatever increase of value one of them gains, must necessarily be lost by the other, and vice versâ, it follows that the value of the object, to which the two others are equal, must be constant.

---

greater quantity of cloth would be given. Why have I not a right to apply your formula to my case of cloth and say that because a greater quantity of cloth is given to the labourer it would fall[14] in value and[15] 100 pieces of cloth will command 7.3[16]

[VI] 31. « But if it can be shown . . . must be lost by *X* ».

A piece of cloth is 120 yards long and is to be divided between *A* and *B*, it is obvious that if you give *A* 100 yards be will have 20, and if you give *A* 60 *B* also will have 60, and that in all cases the two quantities together will make 120. This will be true altho' the value of the whole 120 yards should be £100, £50 or £5. But is it[1] not a begging of the question to assume the constant value because the

14 Replaces 'rise'.
15 'comm' is cancelled here, evidently an interrupted word.
16 The Note breaks off at this point.
1 Inserted.

Now it has ap-|peared that the variable values of the labour and of the profits which compose the value of the variable quantity of corn awarded in wages to a given number of labourers, must necessarily be such, that, as the quantity of labour required to produce them increases, either from difficulty of production or from the greater quantity of produce awarded to the labourer, all the value thus gained by labour is lost by profits; and as the quantity of labour required to produce them is diminished, either by facility of production or the small quantity of produce awarded to the labourer, all the value which is gained by profits is lost by labour. Consequently, the value of the variable quantity of produce which, under different circumstances, forms the wages of a given number of men, being composed of the values of the two elements, labour and profits, varying as above described, must be constant, and may therefore, with propriety, be proposed as a standard measure. **[VII]** (32)

I have entered at some length into the details which show the necessary constancy of the value of labour, on account of its great importance; but, in reality, it follows directly from the manner in which the natural value of commodities and of wages is estimated, that | when the labourer earns a (33)
greater or a smaller quantity of money or necessaries, it is not the value of

---

quantity is constant and because it is always to be divided between 2 persons[(2)].

This is the only passage in which a reason is given for[(3)] the value of labour being the standard measure of value, and never was there a less logical proof of a proposition advanced. If the value be constant how can profits and wages both rise see Page 41[(4)].

[VII][(1)] 100 yds. of Cloth are of £100 value, of which 20 is paid to the clothier for the profits on his capital, and 80 to the workmen for their labour.

[2] This paragraph, with minor alterations, was inserted by Ricardo in his letter to Malthus of 29 April 1823 (*Works*, vol. IX, p. 283).

[3] 'supposing' is cancelled here.

[4] Compare Malthus's page 41, 2nd paragraph, below, p. 36. This last sentence is inserted. In his *Notes on Malthus* of 1820, Ricardo had insisted that profits and wages cannot both rise. See, for an instance of this, his Note 2, *Works*, vol. II, p. 9.

[1] No page reference is given by Ricardo. This Note is written on the back of a letter dated 6 May 1823.

labour which varies, but, as Adam Smith says, "it is the goods which are cheap in the one case and dear in the other."

If labour alone, without any capital, were employed in procuring the fruits of the earth, the greater facility of procuring one sort of them compared with another, would not, it is acknowledged, alter the value of labour, or the exchangeable value of the whole produce obtained by a given quantity of exertion. We should, without hesitation, allow that the difference was in the cheapness or dearness of the produce, not of the labour.

In the same manner it will follow, that when capital and profits enter into the computation of value, and the demand for labour varies, the high or low reward of labour estimated in produce, implies a change in the value of the produce, not a change in the value of the labour.

If the increased reward of the labourer takes place without an increase of produce, this cannot happen without a fall of profits, as it is a self-evident truth, that given the quantity of the produce to be divided between labour and profits, the greater the portion of it which goes to labour the less will be
(34) left for profits. What then will be the result? It will appear | that the value of the produce has fallen, and the value of wages, or of labour, will have remained the same. To obtain any given portion of the produce the same quantity of labour is necessary as before, but profits being diminished, the value of the produce is decreased; while this diminution of profits in

---

At the same time £100 – will command the labour of 1000 men for one day.

Cloth continues to be produced by the same quantity of labour but in consequence of the[(2)] difficulty of producing corn and corn wages rising[(3)] instead of 100 yards selling for £100 or 1000 days labour they sell[(4)] only for £95 – or 950 days labour. –

At this new value of cloth the workman must receive 84.21 yards in order to get £80, or the same quantity of corn as before, and consequently 15.79 remain for the clothier, worth 15 £.

According to your rule then 84.21 yards of cloth must, after corn has risen, contain the same quantity of labour and profit united which 80 contained before corn rose – let us see whether this is true.

[2] 'rise' is cancelled here. [3] Last four words are inserted.
[4] Replaces 'it sells'.

reference to the value of wages is just counterbalanced by the increased quantity of labour necessary to procure the increased produce awarded to the labourer, leaving the value of labour the same as before.

Perhaps in the case just supposed, the result may be said to be occasioned by a fall in the value of the produce, without what could properly be called an increased demand for labour. But if we suppose that a considerable number of labourers were sent out of the country, or swept off by a plague, there could then be no doubt of a great demand for labour, yet the result would be similar. A larger quantity of produce would necessarily be awarded to the labourer, and profits would fall.**[VIII]** A given quantity of produce obtained by the same quantity of labour as before, would fall in value on account of the fall of that part of its value which consisted of profits, while the fall of profits on the increased wages would be balanced by the increased labour necessary to obtain them. |

If instead of labourers being sent out of the country, labourers were (35)
imported, the result would be just opposite. A smaller quantity of produce would be awarded to the labourer and profits would rise. A given quantity of produce, which had been obtained by the same quantity of labour as

---

In the first case 80 yards of cloth are the produce of 640 men's labour for one day 640

	640
Profits	160
	800

In the second 84.21 yards are the produce of 673

	673
Profits	127
	800

[VIII] 34. If half the inhabitants of England were swept off by a plague, and wages were paid by a much larger quantity of money, of corn, or of any other commodity we should be bound to say according to Mr. Malthus that all those commodities had fallen and that[1] labour had remained invariably of the same value. What is this but an arbitrary assumption of a measure of value[2]?

1 Inserted.

2 Instances of a similar argument are to be found in Ricardo's letter to Malthus of 29 April 1823 (*Works*, vol. IX, p. 282), to Trower of 24 July 1823 (*Works*, vol. IX, p. 319), to Malthus of 3 August 1823 (*Works*, vol. IX, p. 321), in *Absolute Value and Exchangeable Value* (*Works*, vol. IV, p. 408).

before, would rise in value on account of the rise of profits, while this rise of profits, in reference to the wages of the labourer, would be balanced by the smaller quantity of labour necessary to obtain the diminished produce awarded to the labourer.

In the former case of the demand for labour, it appeared that the greater earnings of the labourer were occasioned, not by a rise in the value of labour, but by a fall in the value of the produce for which the labour was exchanged. And in the latter case of the abundance of labour, it appeared that the small earnings of the labourer were occasioned by a rise in the value of the produce, and not by a fall in the value of the labour.

The result would be similar, if instead of supposing the same quantity of produce to be obtained by the same quantity of labour, we were to suppose the greatest variations to take place in the fertility of the soil, and,
(36) consequently, in the productive power of labour. | In all cases it would still be found that, as Adam Smith says, it is the produce which varies in value, not the labour for which it will exchange; and if money were obtained in the way in which its value would unquestionably be the most constant, all these variations would appear in the money prices of commodities, whenever the demand for labour varied; while the money price of a given quantity of labour would remain the same.*

The following Table will further illustrate the necessary constancy in the value of labour, and some of its most important results, in a clearer manner and in a shorter compass than if each case were taken separately.

The first column represents the varying fertility of the soil, by the varying quantity of corn which can be obtained by the labour of a given number of men. |

(37) The second column represents the yearly corn wages of each labourer, determined by the state of the demand and supply of produce compared with labour.

The third column represents the variable advances of produce, in the form of corn wages, which, according to the rate at which the labourers are paid, are necessary to obtain the produce of the first column.

The fourth column represents the rate of profits determined in the

* Mr. Ricardo, by supposing gold to be produced always by a certain quantity of labour and *capital*, is compelled to acknowledge that his standard "would be a perfect measure of value for all things produced under the same circumstances precisely as itself, but for no others." p. 43. This concession appears to me quite fatal. We want to measure the value of commodities under *all circumstances*, and it is only gold obtained exclusively by labour, or labour itself, which can do this. See *Principles of Political Economy considered with a View to their Practical Application*, pp. 111 and 118.

common way, by the proportion which the excess of the produce in the first column above the produce paid to the labourers in the third, bears to these advances.

The fifth and sixth columns represent the quantity of labour required to produce the varying corn wages of the given number of men, with the profits estimated also in quantity of labour; and the reader will see at once that these two columns must necessarily, from the manner in which profits and wages are estimated, make up the constant quantity and value of labour which appears in the seventh column.

The eighth and ninth columns show the value of a given quantity of corn, and the value of the produce of a given number of men under the varying circumstances supposed. |

The first and most important truth illustrated in the table is, that, from (39)
the division of value into labour and profits, and the mode in which profits are always estimated, it follows necessarily, that the quantity of labour required to produce the wages of a given number of men, with the addition of the profits upon these advances estimated in labour, must always be exactly the same as the quantity of labour which the wages will command, and must together always make up the constant quantity which appears in the seventh column. But the quantity of labour required to produce the varying wages of ten men is, under the different circumstances supposed, very different, as appears in the fifth column; and it is obvious, that while the numbers in the fifth column vary, the numbers in the seventh column, or the quantity of labour and profits united, cannot be constant, unless, as the quantity of labour required to produce the wages of ten men increases, the quantity of profits estimated in labour diminishes exactly in the same degree. But this, from what has before been stated, must, under the circumstances supposed, be the case. And it follows, that if the natural value of a commodity may be estimated by the labour and profits of which it is
composed, the natural value of the corn | wages of a given number of men (40)
must always be the same. But such wages, according to the postulate with which we commenced, must necessarily be equal to the quantity of labour for which they will exchange. Consequently the value of a given quantity of labour must, under every variety which can take place in the fertility of the soil and the corn wages of labour, be always constant. It is, however, of the greatest importance to remark, that an exact balance of labour, and of profits estimated in labour, so as to yield always a constant quantity, cannot take place in the production of any one commodity or given portion of a commodity; because any one commodity, or given portion of a commodity, is liable to vary in relation to labour, and such variation will either

Table illustrating the invariable Value of Labour and its Results. **[IX]** (38)

1. Quarters of Corn produced by Ten Men, or varying Fertility of the Soil.	2. Yearly Corn Wages to each Labourer, determined by the Demand and Supply.	3. Advances in Corn Wages, or variable Produce commanding the Labour of Ten Men.	4. Rate of Profits under the foregoing Circumstances.	5. Quantity of Labour required to produce the Wages of Ten Men under the foregoing Circumstances.	6. Quantity of Profits on the Advances of Labour.	7. Invariable Value of the Wages of a given Number of Men.	8. Value of 100 Quarters of Corn under the varying Circumstances supposed.	9. Value of the Product of the Labour of Ten Men under the Circumstances supposed.
150 qrs.	12 qrs.	120 qrs.	25 pr. Ct.	8	2	10	8.33	12.5
150	13	130	15.38	8.66	1.34	10	7.7	11.53
150	10	100	50	6.6	3.4	10	10	15
140	12	120	16.66	8.6	1.4	10	7.14	11.6
140	11	110	27.2	7.85	2.15	10	9.09	12.7
130	12	120	8.3	9.23	0.77	10	8.33	10.8
130	10	100	30	7.7	2.3	10	10	13
120	11	110	9	9.17	0.83	10	9.09	10.9
120	10	100	20	8.33	1.67	10	10	12
110	10	100	10	9.09	.91	10	10	11
110	9	90	22.2	8.18	1.82	10	11.1	12.2
100	9	90	11.1	9	1	10	11.1	11.1
100	8	80	25	8	2	10	12.5	12.5
90	8	80	12.5	8.88	1.12	10	12.5	11.25

increase or decrease the amount of the labour and profits united. It is only the varying wages of a given number of men bearing, as the terms imply, a constant relation to labour, which, under any changes in the quantity of labour required to produce them, can still continue of the same natural value. And it is precisely this necessary constancy in the natural value of the varying corn wages of labour, which renders the labour which a commodity will command, a standard | measure both of its natural and exchange- (41)
able value.

[IX][1] Whether 300 qrs. of corn be produced by the labour of 10 men, or 110 qrs., provided 100, or any other smaller quantity be in both cases paid for wages the value of corn in Mr. M's measure of value would be the same: For in all circumstances the value would be ascertained by the quantity paid to the 10 labourers. When out of any quantity, the produce of the labour of 10 men, 120 qrs. be given to the labourers, the way to ascertain the value of 100 qrs. by Mr. M's formula is as follows[2]. If 120 qrs. be of the value of 10 days labour of what value is 100 qrs.? When 110 qrs. are paid to the labourers, then we must say, if 110 qrs. be of the value of 10 days labour, of what value will 100 qrs. be? and this is to be rule whether the 10 men actually produce 130, 140, 300, or 500 qrs. and under all the possible variations in the rate of profits.

Now here is the great difference between Mr. M's system and mine, I always estimate the value of corn by a comparison of the whole quantity produced by a given quantity of labour, with such quantity of labour, and not that part only of the whole produce which is paid to the labourers. If 300 qrs. were produced by the labour of 10 men at one time, and at another only 150 qrs. were produced by the same quantity of labour I should say corn had fallen one half in value although there should have been the constant quantity of 120 qrs. paid to the labourers. Mr. M would say that under so great a variation in the quantity of produce and the facility of producing it[3] the value of it had continued uniformly the same.

1 No page reference is given by Ricardo.
2 First written, 'to ascertain its value by Mr. M's formula is', and then modified to read as it does in the text.
3 Last six words are inserted.

2dly. It appears from the Table, that given the produce obtained by ten men, then as corn wages rise, the value of the produce will fall, or command less labour; and the constant value of the advances in labour absorbing a larger proportion of the value of the produce, profits will fall in proportion. But when more is produced by the same number of persons, then unless the corn wages rise so high as exactly to balance it, the value of the whole produce is increased, and the rate of profits and corn wages may both rise at the same time. Thus while the produce is 130 quarters, as labour rises from ten to twelve quarters, profits fall in an opposite direction from 30 per cent. to 8.3. per cent.; but if we compare the wages of labour when the produce is 130 quarters, with the wages of labour when the produce is 150, it appears that labour may rise from twelve to thirteen quarters, at the same time that profits rise from 8.3. to 15.38.

A third result illustrated in the Table is, that labour being constant, all commodities into which profits enter, which may be said to be nearly the whole mass, must fall on the fall of profits, and among these will, of course,
(42) be found | metallic money. Supposing, therefore, money always to require in its production the same quantity of labour and capital, it will regularly fall in value in the progress of cultivation and population; while labour being uniform in value will rise in money price,* and the demand for corn increasing, compared with the demand for labour, the money price of corn will probably rise still more. But if the labourers were paid at all times exactly the same quantity of corn, (which, however, cannot be the case,) the value of corn, like the value of wages, would be constant, and the variations of fertility would only show themselves in the enormous variations of profits.

Thus, when labour is paid at ten quarters each man, the numbers in the eighth column, or the value of a given quantity of corn, must, it is obvious, always be the same, whatever be the quantity produced; and when the land is fertile, the small quantity of labour required to produce ten quarters is balanced by the great profits which appear in the fourth column. |

(43) In the actual state of things, corn generally rises in the progress of cultivation, not only nominally, but really, as may be seen in the eighth column, while labour, it is evident, can only rise nominally.

A fourth result shown in the Table is, that the value of the corn obtained

* It is this rise in the money price of labour, occasioned by the fall of profits, which Mr. Ricardo considers as that necessary rise in the *value* of labour on which he makes so much depend in his system; but if the foregoing reasoning be well founded, it follows that this rise is not a rise in the *value* of labour, but a fall in the value of money.

by ten men depends mainly upon the rate of profits, which again depends mainly upon the demand and supply of corn compared with labour. If corn be in such demand, that notwithstanding the fertility of the soil, a small quantity of it comparatively will purchase the labour required, profits will be very high, and the value of the produce will greatly exceed the constant value of the wages of the labour advanced; but if the supply of corn be so great, compared with labour, that a large quantity of it is required to purchase the given quantity of labour, profits will be low, and the excess of the value of the produce above the constant value of the advances in wages will be inconsiderable.

Thus, when the produce is 150 quarters, if corn be in such plenty that each labourer is awarded thirteen quarters, the profits of stock will be only 15.38 per cent.; and this rate of profit, added to the constant value of the advances in labour, which are represented by 10, | will make the natural value of the (44)
produce equal to 11.53. But if corn, notwithstanding the fertility of the soil, be only supplied in such quantities, compared with labour, as to award the labourer no more than ten quarters, the rate of profits, instead of 15.38 per cent., will be 50 per cent., and the value of the produce, instead of being 11.53, will be 15.

This shows how greatly the natural value of commodities depends upon the average state of the demand and supply, and completely confirms the position in my last work, that the only difference between natural and market prices is, that the former are regulated by the average and ordinary relations of the demand to the supply, and the latter, when they differ from the former, upon the accidental and extraordinary relations of the demand to the supply.

Fifthly, it follows, from the constant value of labour, that,

Given the value of money in different countries, the natural price of commodities, in which the same quantities of labour have been employed, will depend upon the rate and quantity of profits.

Given the rate and quantity of profits, and the value of money, the natural prices of commodities in different countries will depend | upon the (45)
quantity of labour employed upon them.

And given the quantity of labour employed on them, and the rate and quantity of profits, the natural prices of commodities will depend upon the value of money.

But in reality none of the ingredients of natural or money price are given, excepting the natural value of labour, and consequently the money prices of commodities which regulate the ordinary rate at which different countries exchange their commodities with each other, will be determined partly by the quantity of labour employed upon them, partly by the ordinary rate of profits, and partly by the value of money.

The value of metallic money, it has before been stated, while it continues to be obtained by the same quantity of labour and capital, must always fall with the fall of profits, and will consequently have a strong tendency to fall with the progress of cultivation and improvement; but as few nations comparatively have mines of their own, the supplies which they obtain of the precious metals must be purchased by their exportable commodities; and these are produced and exported under such a variety of circumstances,
(46) in respect to cost, and the value of the same | amount of the precious metals is further so much affected by the demand for corn and labour, the state of credit, paper currencies, taxation, and other circumstances, that no rule can safely be laid down on the subject.

Generally the value of money is the lowest in the richest and most manufacturing countries; but this is not always the case; and a country which raises an abundance of raw produce at a small expense of labour and profits, while its money value is kept up by a ready sale for it in foreign markets, and a continued demand for labour, may have the value of its money very low, although it is not rich or manufacturing. This is the case with the United States of America, where, owing to the low value of money, or high money price of labour, there are no doubt some commodities which, though produced by a less value of labour and profits, cannot be exported to England on account of the higher value of money in England; while we know that there are many other products which are obtained by so much a smaller quantity of labour and profits as more than to counterbalance the higher value of money in England, or the higher money price of labour in the United States.

(47) In the same manner there are no doubt many | commodities which, though obtained in England by a much less quantity of labour and profits than in India, cannot be exported to that country on account of the very high value of money in India; while, on the other hand, there are a few commodities in England in which the saving of labour and the effects of capital and skill have been so great, as to allow of their exportation from a country where the money wages of labour are two shillings a day, to one where they are only fourpence; that is, from a country where the value of money is six times lower than in the country to which the commodities are sent.

On the same principle, commodities may be imported from India into England, although the same commodities might be produced in England by a much less quantity of labour and profits, the low value of money in

England more than compensating the greater quantity of labour and profits employed in India.

It is evident, therefore, that the values which determine what commodities shall be exported, and what imported, depend, as before stated, partly upon the quantity of labour employed in their production, partly upon the ordinary rates of profits in each country, and partly upon the value of money. |

A sixth result illustrated in the Table is the important distinction between (48)
cost and value. The two last columns show the value of a given quantity of corn, and the value of the product of a given quantity of labour, under all the variations which may be supposed of fertility and corn wages. The difference between the numbers in the last column, and the uniform number expressing the value of labour, shows exactly the difference between the value of the labour which has been employed upon a production, or its cost, and the labour which that production will command, or its natural and exchangeable value; which, where profits and wages are alone concerned, must be exactly equal to the additional value occasioned by the amount of profits.

The reader will be aware that neither the preceding Table, nor any thing which has been said, tends in any degree to contradict the acknowledged truth that different *kinds* of labour are of very different natural and exchangeable value. It will be further allowed, that even the same kind of labour, and the kind which has been especially referred to, namely common agricultural labour, may, under particular circumstances, and in particular places, vary in value from a partial or temporary state | of demand and (49)
supply. We well know, that, from a partial and temporary demand at a particular period of the year, summer wages are of a very different value from winter wages; but in reality summer wages form a very important part of the wages of the whole year. They are generally employed to pay the rent of the house, or to purchase the necessary clothing for the family. They could not be essentially diminished, without altering the condition of the labourer throughout the year, or the rate of the increase of population. And if the labourer earned a smaller quantity of corn throughout the year, with an undiminished produce, it appears from the Table that the value of that corn would still remain the same, owing to the increased value of those profits of which it was in part composed.

With regard to the variations in the value of labour in different parts of the same country, if they are not partial, or temporary, and consequently exceptions to the general average, they are all resolvable into those differences in the value of money, which unquestionably take place in

different parts of the same country, and arise from a want of demand for
(50) corn and labour, and a want of commodities to exchange | with those parts of the country which are richer in the precious metals.

Having obtained a measure of the value of commodities in their more simple forms, we may apply this measure to the ingredients which compose the most complicated productions, and estimate all the advances which consist of accumulated profits, rents, tithes, and taxes in labour. In the case of taxes on the wages of labour, or an increase in the prices of those other necessaries of the labourer, besides food, which may occasion the sale of a greater quantity of the produce, in order to pay the same number of labourers, as these increased advances will have the same effect upon profits as a simple increase of wages, they will in no respect interfere with the constant value of labour, though an increase of wages, under such circumstances, will be of no advantage to the labourer.

Cases will of course frequently occur, in which the advances which do not consist of wages vary in a different degree from wages; but still the value of labour will remain constant. If the produce, instead of being obtained by the direct labour of a certain number of men, were obtained by the direct
(51) labour of | only a part of this number, together with an amount of materials, or other advances consumed in the same time, equal to the labour of the other part, then upon a rise in the corn wages of labour, if the other advances were to fall, or not to be worth so much labour as before, it is obvious that the profits of stock would not fall so much as if the same rise of corn wages had taken place, when all the advances had been in labour; and it might be thought at first that profits not falling in proportion to the rise of labour, the value of labour would not continue the same. But it will be observed, that, in all cases of this kind, there will be a less value of labour, which is equivalent to a less quantity of it employed to obtain the same produce; and a less quantity of labour altogether being consequently necessary to produce the food of the labourer, than if labour alone had been employed, the higher profits, or smaller diminution of the former profits, will only just be such as to maintain labour of a constant value.

Let us suppose, for instance, that 120 quarters of corn are produced by ten men. If each man were paid ten quarters, profits would be 20 per cent.; and if wages were increased to eleven quarters, profits would fall from 20 per |
(52) cent. to 9.09 per cent. Now supposing, that, instead of ten men being directly employed, five only are so employed, and that the other advances consist of capital which will continue of the same value as the corn;* then,

* This applies to the seed, and the food of the working cattle in agriculture.

while each labourer earns ten quarters, and the other capital advanced is worth the labour of five men so paid, profits will be, as before, 20 per cent. But if the labourer be paid eleven quarters instead of ten, profits will not fall, as before, from 20 per cent. to 9.09 per cent., but only from 20 per cent. to 14.28 per cent.; because the advances, instead of being 110, will only be 105; and the value of these advances estimated in labour paid at eleven quarters each man, being only 9.54, instead of 10; 9.54 may be considered as the number of persons employed. Then if 120 quarters be produced by 9.54 men, 105 quarters will be produced by 8.34. But 8.34, increased by a profit of 14.28, will make 9.54, the quantity of labour employed, and show that the natural value of labour is always proportioned to its quantity. In the former case, when ten men were employed at eleven quarters, as the advances | were 110 quarters, instead of 105, the labour required to produce (53)
the food of the labourer was 9.166, and consequently a profit of only 9.09 will be sufficient to make up ten, the number of men employed, and thus equalize the value with the quantity.

In the case of fixed capital of considerable duration, there is always a probability that it will alter in value in reference to the quantity of labour, and of profits estimated in labour, of which it was composed when first produced; but after having advanced so far in establishing the labour which a commodity will command, as the measure of its value, we are entitled to consider the present value estimated in labour of any fixed capital which is about to be employed in production, as representing the quantity of accumulated labour actually so applied. It is further necessary, as before stated, to reckon the remaining value of the fixed capital as a part of the produce resulting from the whole of the accumulated and immediate labour employed. When, however, these corrections have been made, all the cases in which fixed capital enters, which may be said to include the great mass of commodities, will be found to answer to the theory as accurately as the simplest case that can be stated. |

The exceptions, therefore, to the general proposition that the labour (54)
which commodities will command may be considered as a standard measure of their value are only apparent, not real, and may all be consistently explained.

And if the proposition be true, a standard measure of value is of so much importance in political economy, and the one proposed is at all times so very ready and easy of application,* that there is scarcely any part of the science in which it will not tend to simplify and facilitate our inquiries.

* The labour worked up in a commodity could not, in many cases, be ascertained without considerable difficulty; but the labour which it will command is always open and palpable.

To advert shortly to a few points on which there have been some differences of opinion.

On the subject of rents, such a standard would determine, among other things, that, as the increase in the *value* of corn is only measured by a decrease in the corn wages of labour, such increase of value is a very inconsiderable source of the increase of rents compared with improvements in agriculture; and on the same principle that, if tithes do not fall mainly on the labourer, the acknowledged diminution in the *corn* rents of the
(55) landlord, | occasioned by tithes, cannot be balanced by an increase of their value, and that, consequently, tithes must fall mainly on the landlord.**[X]**

On the subject of labour it would determine, that the increasing *value* of the funds destined for the maintenance of labour can alone occasion an increase in the demand for it, or the will and power to employ a greater number of labourers; and that it is consistent with theory, as well as general experience, that high corn wages, in proportion to the quantity of work done, should frequently occur with a very slack demand for labour;* or, in other words, that when the *value* of the whole produce falls from excess of supply compared with the demand, it cannot have the power of setting the same number of labourers to work.**[XI]**

* Practically, in all countries such as South America and Ireland, where there is a slack demand for labour, and the people are but half employed, the food wages of labour are high, compared with the work done.

[X] 54 According to Mr. Malthus a landlord is a sufferer from tithes if he has a diminished corn rent because he cannot command so much labour, Mr. M's standard of value; But would he be a sufferer, if it could be proved, which it can be, that though[1] he may not be able to command so much labour as before he can command as much[2] cloth, shoes, hats, sugar[3] money and all other commodities whatever.

[XI] 55 As Mr. M defines value to be measured by the power of commanding labour, and therefore the increasing value of the funds destined for the maintenance of labour must mean the increasing power of commanding labour. The proposition is undoubtedly a

[1] 'it may be possible that' is cancelled here.
[2] 'as much' replaces 'more'.
[3] 'malt' is cancelled here.

On the subject of profits, it would show, that they are determined, not by the varying value of a given quantity of labour compared with the constant value of the commodities which it produces, but, as is more conformable to | our experience, by the variable value of the commodities produced by a given quantity of labour, compared with the constant value of such labour; and that profits never, on any occasion, rise or fall, unless the value of the produce of a given quantity of labour rises or falls, either from the temporary or ordinary state of the demand and supply.**[XII]** (56)

On the subject of the distinction between wealth and value, it would show, that though they are by no means the same, they are much more closely connected than they have of late been supposed to be; and that the best practical measure of the relative wealth of different countries would be the quantity of common labour which the value of the whole annual produce of each country would enable it to command at the actual price of the time, which in some rich countries might amount to above double the number of families actually employed, and in poor countries might not greatly exceed such number.**[XIII]**

On the subject of foreign trade, it would show that its universally

---

true and a safe one which says that the increase of the[1] power of commanding labour depends upon the increase of the funds with which labour is paid.

« Or in other words etc. » that is to say it is consistent with theory that when the power of employing labour (Mr. M's name for value) diminishes, so much labour will not be employed.

[1] Last three words replace 'increasing'.

[XII] 56 What can be meant by the words « compared with the[1] constant value of labour » Labour is the measure, the standard, its value cannot be otherwise than constant.

[1] Last three words are inserted.

[XIII] 56+ With the same quantity of commodities that country would be the richest whose labourers[1] were satisfied with the coarsest food and necessaries.

[1] Replaces 'inhabitants'.

acknowledged effect in giving a stimulus to production, generally, is mainly owing to its increasing the value of the produce of a country's labour by the
(57) extension of demand, before the value of its labour | is increased by the increase of its quantity; and that the effect of every extension of demand, whether foreign or domestic, is always, as far as it goes, to increase the average rate of profits* till this increase is counteracted by a further accumulation of capital.

On the subject of the accumulation of capital it would show that if the increase of capital be measured by the increase of its materials, such as corn, clothing, &c., then it is obvious that the supply of these materials may, by saving, increase so rapidly, compared with labour and the wants of the effective demanders, that with a greater quantity of materials the capitalist will neither have the power nor the will to set in motion the same quantity of labour, and that consequently the progress of wealth will be checked; but that if the increase of capital be measured, as it ought to be, by the increase of its power to command labour, then accumulation so limited cannot possibly go on too fast.

(58) On the general subject of demand and sup-|ply, it would show that they must be restored to their universal empire, both in reference to the prices of commodities, and the dependence of the progress of wealth on the due proportion maintained between them. If the cost of a commodity be considered as composed exclusively of the actual advances of the capital required for its production, which seems to be the most natural and correct mode of viewing it,† then it is obvious, that as both the prices and values of commodities are proportioned to these advances, with the *addition* of profits very variable in their amount, neither of them can be determined by these advances alone, or by the costs of production so defined. We must therefore have recourse to demand and supply. And on the other hand, if profits be included in the costs of production, then, as it follows, from the constancy of the value of labour, that ordinary profits are determined by the ordinary demand compared with the ordinary supply of the products of the same
(59) quantity of labour, the certain conclusion must be, that | demand and supply enter powerfully into the costs of production according to this latter

* If profits rise in some departments without falling proportionally in others, the *average* rate of profits will have increased, although, from the difficulty of moving capital, the rate of profits in some employments may not have had time to rise before the stimulus to such rise comes to an end by a fresh increase of capital.

† This is the view taken of it by Colonel Torrens in his *Production of Wealth*, which I think the just one; because it makes the proper distinction between cost and value, on which the great stimulus to production depends. But he has most unnecessarily and incorrectly given the same interpretation to *natural price*, which always includes profits.

definition, and that therefore their dominion as to prices and value is absolutely universal.*

Nor would they be less so in their effect on the general progress of wealth. If commodities and the materials of capital increase faster than the effectual demand for them, profits fall prematurely, and capitalists are ruined without a proportionate benefit to the labouring classes, because an increasing demand for labour cannot go on under such circumstances. If the value of commodities and the materials of capital increase for some time without an increase of their quantity, the labouring classes must soon be supported on the lowest amount of food on | which they will consent to (60) keep up their actual number; and the main part of the population would suffer severely without any proportionate benefit to the capitalists; because the value of their capitals, measured by the labour which they can command, would shortly be incapable of further increase. In either of these cases a decided check would be given to the progress of wealth, which progress must necessarily be the greatest, when the joint product of the capitalist and labourer, which the state of the land and the skill with which it is worked enable them to obtain, is so divided between them, that in the progress of cultivation and improvement any unnecessary or premature fall either of profits or corn wages is prevented. But this can only be accomplished by a proper proportion of the supply to the demand, that is, by an accumulation so proportioned to the actual consumption of produce by those who can make an effectual demand for it, as to occasion the greatest permanent annual increase in the value of the materials of capital.

The reader of my last work, in which I laid down as my rule, to admit no principles of Political Economy as just which were inconsistent with general experience, will be aware that the conclusions to which I have here shortly ad-|verted, as following necessarily from the constancy of the value of (61) labour, are almost exactly the same as the conclusions of that work. And the reason is, that although at that time I did not think that the labour which a commodity would command could, with propriety, be considered as a

* In order to exclude demand and supply from the costs of production, when ordinary profits are considered as making a part of them, it would be necessary to assume that the corn wages of labour are always the same, an assumption which would be quite unwarranted, not only in reference to short periods, but to periods of fifty or sixty years, as the history of corn wages in this country alone amply testifies (see ch. iv. sect. 4, of my Princ. of Pol. Econ. &c.); and what but the state of the demand and supply of corn, compared with labour, prevents profits in the United States from being 100 per cent.? The quantity of corn divided between the labourer and capitalist would be amply sufficient to yield such profits, if the corn wages of labour were no higher than in England.

standard measure of value, yet I thought it the nearest approximation to a standard of any one object known, and consequently applied it, on almost all occasions, to correct the errors arising from the application of more variable measures. The conclusions, therefore, of my former and present reasonings were likely to be nearly the same, although the premises might now admit of further correction and illustration, and the conclusions might be pronounced with greater precision and certainty.

It was my intention to have done this much more fully than in the present treatise; but having been interrupted by unforeseen circumstances, and being unwilling to delay any longer the publication of this essential part of my proposed plan, I have determined to submit it to the public in its present form; and will only add here a few observations on a question closely connected with it, which has lately excited much interest and discussion. |

(62) Among the questions for the determination of which a standard measure of value is most particularly required, are those which relate to alterations in the value of the currency. We know perfectly well, from experience, that commodities are subject to great variations of price, and that many of these variations may arise from causes which alter the natural value of these commodities, and are equally applicable to a large mass of them, as to a very few. On the supposition of a large mass being altered, any article which had retained the same natural value, would have its power of purchasing considerably affected; but this would be owing to an alteration in the value of the mass of commodities, and not in the value of the article, which by the supposition remains the same. It follows, that although money may increase in its power of purchasing, it does not necessarily increase in value. But in estimating the value of money, some criterion or other must be referred to. If we cannot refer to the mass of commodities, we must refer to some one object, and this object can only be labour. Our present inquiry, therefore, must be into the causes which affect the value of the precious metals as compared with labour.

(63) These causes are of two kinds: – first, those | which occasion a high or low rate of profits, which, as connected with the progressive cultivation of poorer land, and operating universally and necessarily on the precious metals in common with all other commodities, and raising or lowering them with regard to labour, may be denominated the primary and necessary cause of the high or low value of metallic money. – And secondly, those which depend on the fertility and vicinity of the mines; the different efficiency of labour in different countries; the abundance or scarcity of exportable commodities; and the state of the demand and supply of commodities and labour compared with money; which may be denomi-

nated the secondary and incidental causes of the high or low value of metallic money.

These two different kinds of causes will sometimes act in conjunction, and sometimes in opposition, so that it may not always be easy to distinguish their separate effects; but as these effects have really a different origin, it is desirable to keep them as separate as we can.

The marks which distinguish a fall in the value of the precious metals, arising from the primary cause, are, – a rise in the money price of raw produce and labour, without a general rise in the price of wrought commodities. All of them, indeed, as far as they are com-|posed of raw (64)
produce, will have a tendency to rise; but, in a large class of commodities, this tendency to rise will be more than counterbalanced by the effect of the fall of profits. – Some therefore will rise, and some will fall, as I stated in my last work,* according to the nature of the capitals employed upon them, compared with those which produce money; and while the money prices of corn and labour very decidedly increase, the prices of commodities, taken on the average, may possibly remain not far from the same.

On the other hand, when the value of metallic money falls, from the secondary causes above noticed, there will be a tendency to a proportionate rise of all commodities as well as of corn and labour, though in some cases it may take a considerable time before it is completely effected. And, in general, whenever a fall in the value of money takes place, without a fall in the rate of profits, an event which is generally open to observation, it is to be attributed to incidental and secondary causes affecting the relations of money to labour, and not to that which is connected with the taking of poorer land into cultivation.

Of these two classes of causes the second | produces much the greatest part (65)
of those differences in the value of metallic money, which are the most observable in different countries, and at different periods in the same country. If India and England had each of them mines of equal natural fertility, the superior efficiency of English labour, assisted by machinery, would extract a much greater quantity of metal from such mines; and the money price of labour might be three or four times higher, and the value of money three or four times lower in England than in India.**[XIV]**

The same effect is, at present, practically produced by the skill and

* Sect. IV. p. 91, et seq.

[XIV] 65 Not if there were a free trade between the two countries.

machinery employed on the manufactures with which England purchases her gold. If she can prepare exportable commodities which are in demand abroad, with much less labour than other nations, she will be able to buy gold at a much lower natural value, and will continue to import it under favourable exchanges, till its value falls in proportion.

It is farther established by experience, that a brisk or slack demand for commodities and labour, and particularly for corn, has a considerable effect on the value of gold. Such a demand not only occasions a more rapid
(66) circulation of money, and enables the same quantity | to perform a greater number of transactions, but calls into action a greater quantity of credit and private paper,* so that a general rise of bullion prices, including labour, seems to be at all times possible, even without any fresh importations of the precious metals; and the only practical limit to this rise, is the turn of the exchange, and the impossibility of maintaining the exchanges nearly at par beyond a certain elevation of labour and commodities.

The secondary and incidental causes here enumerated, as affecting the value of gold, often completely overcome the effects arising from the primary cause. The state of bullion prices in most of the countries of the commercial world make it evident, that the efficiency of labour, and the abundance of exportable commodities, are much more powerful in lowering the value of bullion in the countries where they prevail, than high profits in raising it; and the same appears to be true, in reference to an increased demand for corn and labour.

* One of the most valuable sections in Mr. Tooke's late work *On High and Low Prices*, is the seventh, in which he proves the frequent occurrence of this event, and explains, with great clearness and knowledge of the subject, the mode in which it takes place.

[XV] 67 Did you always think that during the greatest part of the war bullion fell in value?[(1)]

[1] Cp. Ricardo's comment on Malthus's *Principles* in *Works*, vol. II, Note 85, pp. 150–1.

[XVI]

« . . . this low rate of profits would have a natural tendency to raise the bullion price of labour; . . . ».

67 Do you not consider a low rate of profit and a small power of commanding labour with profits as synonymous?

It cannot be doubted that the rate of interest | and profits was comparatively high during the late war, and this high rate of profits would naturally have a tendency to lower the bullion price of labour; but this was more than counterbalanced by the tendency of a brisk demand for corn and labour to raise money prices generally, including labour, and the consequence was a fall, during the greatest part of the time, in the value of bullion.**[XV]** (67)

It can as little be doubted, that the rate of interest and profits has fallen since the war, and this low rate of profits would have a natural tendency to raise the bullion price of labour;**[XVI]** but this has been more than counterbalanced by the tendency of a slack demand for corn and labour to lower prices generally, and the consequence has been a rise in the value of gold, and a still greater rise in the value of the currency.**[XVII]**

This rise, however, in the value of the currency, has been by no means so considerable as those are inclined to make it, who would measure it by the fall of agricultural produce; nor is it so inconsiderable as those imagine who would measure it solely by the difference between paper and gold. But whether this difference is the whole of what can be fairly attributed to the Bank Restriction and the re-|turn to cash payments, or not, it may by no (68) means be the whole change which has taken place in the value of the currency, when compared with an object which has not changed.

It would be very desirable to be able to form an accurate estimate of the

---

[XVII][1] Might I not express this paragraph in[2] the following words

It can as little be doubted that the rate of interest and profits has[3] fallen since the war, and this diminished power of employing labour, with the profits on a given amount of capital,[4] would have a natural tendency to increase the rewards of labour[5]; but this has been more than counterbalanced by the tendency of a slack demand for corn and labour to lower prices generally, and the consequence has been an increase in the power of gold to employ labour, and a still greater increase in the power of employing labour in the currency.

[1] No page reference is given by Ricardo.
[2] Last four words replace 'put this paragraph into'.
[3] Replaces 'had'.
[4] Last eight words replace 'a given amount of profits'.
[5] Last five words replace 'raise the bullion price of labour', which however is not cancelled, but is included in parentheses.

rise and fall which has taken place in the bullion price of labour for the last thirty years; but unfortunately, during the latter part of the period, no general estimates of the price of labour have been made, at least none that have come to my knowledge; and there is reason to think that, under the late stagnation in the demand for agricultural labour, the common rate of wages in England has been more than usually interrupted by the operation of the poor laws. On this account, I have made some inquiries respecting wages in Scotland, and have obtained a most valuable communication; but before I refer to it particularly, it may be useful to consider the results of the data we possess in England. The rise in the bullion price of labour from 1790 to 1810 and 11, may be established upon satisfactory grounds, although the amount of the fall which has since taken place may be a matter of considerable uncertainty.

According to the communications to the Board of Agriculture, the price
(69) of labour, in | 1790, was 8*s.* 1*d.* per week. In 1796, Sir F. M. Eden, in his work on the Poor, stated it at 8*s.* 11*d.* per week. In 1803, the communications to the Board of Agriculture make it 11*s.* 5*d.*, and in 1810 and 11, according to satisfactory returns obtained by Arthur Young, it was 14*s.* 6*d.*★ This was a steady and very great rise in the price of agricultural labour during the course of twenty years. But in 1810 and 11, paper had separated from gold to a considerable extent. Taking an average of the market prices of gold during these two years, this price was £4. 13*s.* and reducing the 14*s.* 6*d.* currency to a bullion price, it will appear that the bullion wages of labour in 1810 and 11 were a little above 12*s.* The bullion price of labour had therefore risen 50 per cent. Now, on the supposition that manufacturing and mercantile labour continued to bear the same proportion to agricultural labour as before,† it is obvious that there would be a difference of 50 per
(70) cent. | between the quantity of labour and profits with which an ounce of gold could be purchased at the former period, compared with the latter; that is, while labour was 8*s.* 1*d.* per week, it would require a piece of muslin, which would command above nine and a half weeks labour, to purchase an ounce of gold; but when wages were 12*s.* per week, a piece of muslin, which would command little more than six and a half weeks labour, would be sufficient for the purpose. The natural value of bullion, therefore, the quantity of English labour and profits of which it was composed, must have fallen to that extent.

★ Inquiry into the Rise of Prices in Europe, p. 15.

† Perhaps at the time specifically adverted to, this supposition will not be allowed. But it is always assumed as a general proposition; and although 1810 and 11 were years of great manufacturing distress, yet Mr. Tooke himself brings evidence which shows that manufacturing labour was particularly high in 1805 and 6.

Mr. Tooke, in his late valuable publication, after stating very justly that an unusual proportion of unfavourable seasons must have had a considerable effect in raising the prices of corn and labour during the period adverted to, goes on to "ask upon what ground of fact or reasoning can the high prices included in such a period be ascribed, in fairness, to alterations in the currency, beyond the degree indicated by the difference between paper and gold, when, after a sufficient time has elapsed for the subsidence of the extraordinary effects of such an unusual succession of bad seasons, there is a restoration to a level even somewhat lower than that from | which the rise is (71)
assumed to have taken place, and to have continued progressively."

Of the subsidence here alluded to, before 1814, Mr. Tooke has certainly not given proofs sufficiently general; but without dwelling on this point, it appears to me that the question of the fall in the value of the currency including the gold, is exclusively a question of fact, and must be referred to some criterion. It is a very intelligible thing to say that paper has fallen, if it has fallen with regard to the gold which it professes to represent; but it is not intelligible to say that gold has not fallen, when it is acknowledged to have fallen both with regard to its power of purchasing generally, and its power of commanding labour; unless a reference can be made for the proof of it to some more satisfactory criterion. A season of scarcity will make corn dear, and a season of plenty cheap, without necessarily affecting labour in either case, as is shown by Adam Smith, and proved by repeated experience. But if seasons of scarcity occur so frequently as to raise generally the bullion price of labour, it must of necessity be accompanied by a power of purchasing bullion with a smaller quantity of labour and profits; otherwise the event could not | occur. Whenever it does occur, the natural value of bullion (72)
falls.*

The observations here made, with a view to place the controversy respecting the alterations in the currency on its proper ground, and to make the necessary distinction between facts and the causes which may have produced them, apply still more strongly to the publication of Mr. Blake, in much of the reasoning of which I entirely concur. He proposes to prove that it was the gold which rose, and not the paper which fell during the war, although he acknowledges as a matter of fact, that almost all prices, including labour, rose not only in paper but in gold. This has, no doubt, the air of a contradiction, according to all the common modes of estimating the value of money; and it certainly is not removed by showing that the main

* In poor countries a succession of bad seasons sometimes takes place without any rise in the price of labour, and in that case, though there may be a high price of corn, there is no fall in the natural value of money. It will not be purchased with less labour.

cause of these high prices was a great demand compared with the supply of commodities – a cause which, involving as it always does, more transactions
(73) on credit, and a more rapid circulation | of currency, is one of the most legitimate causes of a fall in the value of money.

Mr. Blake, however, is certainly right in his view of the effects of an unfavourable exchange on the price of gold, when it ceases to form a part of the circulation. It is not only possible that from this cause gold might for a time rise in value much beyond the expense of transporting it; but as a matter of fact, this did unquestionably occur at certain periods during the war. There is no account of the price of agricultural labour in England subsequently to 1811. Probably it did not rise any more; but if it did, judging from what took place in Scotland, it did not rise sufficiently to balance the subsequent rise in the market price of gold, which was from £4. 15*s.* in 1811, to £5. 8*s.** in 1813. Consequently, in 1813, as compared with 1811, the value of gold must have risen considerably; and on the supposition that the price of labour did not rise after 1811, it would appear that the natural and exchangeable value of gold, as measured by the standard, rose above 13½ per cent.

The rise of gold from the sudden fall of the exchange in consequence of
(74) Buonaparte's return | from Elba was still more remarkable. The price had been as low, in the spring of 1815, as 4*l.* 9*s.*, and without any known change in the currency price of labour, it rose suddenly to 5*l.* 5*s.*, or 18 per cent.; and consequently, to purchase an ounce of gold it was necessary at that time to give commodities worth 18 per cent. more of agricultural labour than it might have been purchased for a month or two before. Whatever might have been the case with the paper, there could not, on any view of the subject, be the slightest foundation for the supposition of a sudden abundance and cheapness of labour just before the battle of Waterloo. In fact, agricultural labour had not fallen, and manufacturing labour was higher than usual; so that even without considering labour as a standard, it must have been acknowledged, that, of these two objects which had altered in relative value, it was the gold which had risen, not the labour which had fallen.

In attempting to measure the *rise* in the value of the currency since the period of the high prices, we shall be greatly assisted by the following very valuable document respecting the price of labour in the county or stewartry of Kircudbright. It is considered that the prices in this table represent pretty
(75) nearly (though they are rather below) the wages in | other parts of Scotland.

* These averages are taken from Lord Lauderdale's *Further Considerations on the State of the Currency*, published in 1813. Appendix, p. 33.

The labourers have no other allowances whatever except the daily wages specified in the table. In the intermediate years not quoted the wages remained stationary at the rates last mentioned; and when any change took place, the period of such change and the degree of it are regularly stated.

Years.	Rate per day in winter.	Rate per day in summer.	Years.	Rate per day in winter.	Rate per day in summer.
1760	4*d.*	6*d.*	1799	12*d.*	15*d.*
1765	6*d.*	8*d.*	1800	14*d.*	16*d.*
1770	8*d.*	10*d.*	1802	16*d.*	18*d.*
1772	8*d.*	12*d.*	1811	18*d.*	22*d.*
1776	7*d.*	9*d.*	1812	20*d.*	24*d.*
1780	8*d.*	10*d.*	1816	18*d.*	22*d.*
1791	8*d.*	11*d.*	1817	16*d.*	20*d.*
1793	9*d.*	12*d.*	1819	15*d.*	18*d.*
1798	11*d.*	14*d.*	1822	12*d.*	15*d.*

In 1812, farm servants boarded in the house received from 14*l.* to 22*l.* a year; women servants from 5*l.* to 8*l.* At present, (April, 1823,) men receive from 10*l.* to 14*l.*, and women from 3*l.* 10*s.* to 6*l.*

Masons' wages per day were three shillings in 1812, and are now half-a-crown.

All work done by the piece, such as building stone fences, cutting ditches either for fences or drains, making roads, &c. may be | done at a greater (76) reduction of price than the fall in the rate of labour by the day. Work is now performed more frequently by the piece; and the best labourers are employed by the day; while the inferior workmen, and those unable from age, or other causes, to perform a full day's work, are turned over to work by the piece. Agricultural affairs are under such depression, that the work is curtailed, and the competition for work is thereby increased.*

The first thing that strikes us in the table is the very remarkable rise of labour in Scotland from 1760 – much greater than in England, and much greater than in proportion to the rise in the price of corn. This was no doubt owing in part to the comparatively unimproved state of the district in question, and of Scotland in general at the earliest period adverted to. But to go no farther back than 1790, the period with which we commenced in

* For the foregoing valuable table, and the information accompanying it, I am indebted to Mr. Mure, of Kircudbright, through the kind intervention of Mr. M[c]Culloch, of Edinburgh.

England, it appears that the rise from 1790 to 1811, was considerably greater than in England, and nearly in proportion to the rise in the price of wheat. |
(77) If, indeed, we take the price of labour as mentioned in the table for 1812, and compare it with the average price of wheat for the four years from 1812 to 1815 inclusive, during which period the same price of labour seems to have continued, it will appear, that labour, taking summer and winter wages together, rose in the proportion of from 19*s.* to 44*s.*, while wheat rose from 43*s.* in 1792, (according to the average of England and Wales, which commences with that year,) to 88*s.* and therefore labour rose decidedly more than wheat, except in reference to the peculiarly high price of wheat in 1812.

Taking the currency price of labour in Scotland as having risen from 9½*d.* to 22*d.*, and reducing the 22*d.* to its value in bullion, the average price of bullion in that year being 5*l.* 1*s.*, it will appear, that the bullion price of labour in Scotland rose, in the interval between 1790 and 1812, from 9½*d.* to 16½*d.*, or nearly 73 per cent. And consequently, the same quantity of gold for which it would have been necessary to give commodities worth 173 days labour in 1790, might be purchased for 100 days labour in 1812; or the value of the currency estimated in gold might be considered as having fallen in that proportion. |

(78) In 1812, the bullion price of labour as above stated was 16½*d.*; it has since fallen to 13½*d.*, or in the proportion of from 100 to 81·8 – rather more than 18 per cent. This view of it shows most clearly the change in the bullion value of the currency since 1812. But if we wish to estimate the whole fall which has taken place in the currency, and then subtract what is due to the difference between paper and gold, it will appear that the whole fall since 1812, estimated on the currency wages of 1812, has been rather less than 39 per cent.; of which, if the average difference between paper and gold in the year 1812 was as 101 to 78, about 23 per cent. would belong to the paper, leaving about 16 per cent. for the fall in the currency independently of the excess of paper prices above gold prices. The apparent difference in the results of these estimates arises merely from the per centage in the latter case being taken on a higher number.

I stated before, that I was not aware of any data on which reliance could be placed respecting the amount of the fall of agricultural wages in England since the termination of the war; but on the supposition that the wages, which in 1810 and 1811 were 14*s.* 6*d.* per week, had fallen to 10*s.* then as the
(79) bullion wages of 1810 and 1811 were a little above 12*s.*, the | fall in the bullion value of the currency would be nearly 17 per cent., or for the same quantity of gold which in 1810 and 1811 might be purchased by commodi-

ties worth 83 days labour, it would now be necessary to give commodities the natural value of which would be represented by 100 days labour. This difference of course includes the effects which have been attributed to the purchases of bullion by the Bank with a view to a return to cash payments, the amount of which separately it is scarcely possible to calculate; but I am inclined to agree with Mr. Tooke in thinking that it is not above one or two per cent. If the price of agricultural labour in England has not fallen so much as is here supposed, the difference in the value of the currency will not be so great as above stated, but on any supposition which is at all probable, it must be something considerable.

It is certain therefore that the currency, estimated in what appears to be a correct standard of value, has fallen in such a degree beyond the difference between paper and gold, as to add much to the pressure upon the landed interest, though by no means to the extent which would be implied by measuring the value of the currency in agricultural produce. This pro-|duce, (80)
from the scantiness of the supply compared with the demand, was at one time much above its natural and ordinary value, and has since, from the abundance of the supply compared with the demand, been as much below its natural value; while the value of the currency, though it has fallen and risen considerably, has been much more steady than the value of corn.

To what extent the alterations in the value of the currency beyond the difference between bullion and paper are attributable to the Bank restriction, and the return to cash payments, it is by no means easy to say. That the currency would have fallen very considerably under the circumstances of the last war, and risen very considerably under the circumstances which accompanied the peace, although paper had been kept on a par with gold, I cannot feel the least doubt; and probably the only difference has been, that as the increase of paper beyond what would circulate at par with gold gave facilities to production, and to the bringing of poor land into cultivation during the war, it has tended to increase the glut and low prices since the peace.

But whatever may have been the pressure on the owners of land since the peace, they cannot | have the slightest plea for an attempt to indemnify (81)
themselves at the expense of the public creditor. In the turns of the wheel of fortune all parties should have fair play; no class of persons can be justified in endeavouring to lift themselves up by using unfair and dishonourable means to pull others down; and least of all ought such means to be thought of by the landlords of this country, who, whatever inconveniences they may have suffered latterly, have unquestionably altogether benefited much more

largely from the alterations in the value of the currency, than the very persons who in their opinion should be made to relieve them from their embarrassments.

Appendix

A letter of J. Mill to J. R. McCulloch★

E[ast] I[ndia] House
10th Jany 1824

My Dear Sir,

My opinion pretty nearly concurs with yours on all points relating to the lectures†. I do not see how you can do justice to the subject in less than 20 lectures, but you must look to that as your limit. No doubt there ought to be three lectures a week; but I am afraid we must content ourselves with two the *first* year. People here are not accustomed to attend lectures; the evening is the only time they can give; and the calls upon the evening are numerous. But that is a matter fully open to consideration hereafter. – We are all of opinion that women ought *not* to be excluded. – Any time from the beginning of March to the end of June will do. April and May are the very best months; so that you may make your own arrangement, to which we shall conform. I am happy you think of a class of conversation.

As to subscriptions from the members of Mr. Ricardo's family, we deemed it a matter of propriety to keep it out of their way, and indeed to

★ Addressed to: J. R. McCulloch Esq. / Bucklieugh Place / Edinburgh. This letter has been quoted in Professor O'Brien's book on McCulloch (D. P. O'Brien *McCulloch. A Study in Classical Economics*, London: G. Allen & Unwin, 1970, pp. 48, 49, 50 and 136).

MS at the University of London Library (AL 187/25). First published in *Rivista Internazionale di Scienze Economiche & Commerciali* (International Review of Economics and Business), 1979, n. 1, pp. 33–4.

† Ricardo Memorial Lectures (see *Works*, vol. IX, p. 391; also O'Brien, *McCulloch*, *cit.*, ch. 4, pp. 48–57).

give a hint that our desire was to accomplish the object without them. Their feelings towards the business are exactly what they ought to be.

We did not much like the idea of advertising for subscriptions; and never doubted the accomplishment of our purpose in the quieter way. You can have little notion of the dread of publicity which hangs over many of us: and of the aversion to Political Economy which yet is here almost universal. Take this as an example: When Hume* who has a project of his own for a bust and tablet to Ricardo in West. Abbey, asked subscription from Hudson Gurney M.P., he said he would give £50 if needed to the bust, but not one farthing to the lectures. Think of the *terrae filius!* And Huskisson†, when applied to, in like manner, by Hume, slunk away, saying, he was by no means convinced of the utility of such lectures; and besides, in his public situation, he was not yet prepared to like having his name published, as that of a Political Economist. Oh, you coward! said Hume to him. And he replied I must confess it is the right name. Courage, in that sense of the word, seems to be the rarest of human qualities. Could not something be said with a view to these wretched feelings, in the Edin. Rev. Something shall be said in the Morn. Chron. – In due time the lectures will of course be advertised. –

I have been to Brighton to see Mrs. Ricardo, and have seen all the M.S.S. they had there. The plan for the Bank‡ seems to have received his last hand; and as Mr. Moses§, to whom all the papers are confided, is anxious for its publication, and I see no reason against it, this will soon appear. You already know pretty well what it is. There is a good deal written on the subject of value, but rather in scraps, and as thoughts put down as they were excogitated, than in a form for the public. I do not find any thing new, any thing different from the ideas we have heard him throw out. I think it is possible that in some of his letters to you, or to Malthus, his thoughts may be put in a better form, than in the papers I have seen. If so, they ought to be made use of, at least in a detailed account of his life. You have probably seen the account of him in the Annual Obituary, which was written by his brother Moses.**

* Joseph Hume, M.P.

† MS reads 'Huskinson'. Mill refers undoubtedly to William Huskisson, M.P.

‡ *Plan for the Establishment of a National Bank* (quoted above, p. xi, fn.).

§ D. Ricardo's brother.

** *A Memoir of David Ricardo* (From *The Annual Biography and Obituary, for the year 1824*. See also *Works*, vol. X, pp. 3–13). This passage provides conclusive evidence about the authorship of the 'Memoir of Ricardo' and confirms the conjecture contained in the editorial 'Note on the Authorship of the Memoir' (see *Works*, vol. X, pp. 14–15).

I do not recollect any other particular of present importance, and being in a hurry shall conclude with all good wishes from your friend

J. Mill

Index

The present Index registers persons, geographical names, sources and subjects contained in this book. Ricardo and Malthus are not listed in the index.

Absolute value, 8
 and exchangeable value, x, xviii, xx
 Ricardo's paper, x n., xi n., xii, xiii, xiv, xix, 31 n.
Annual Biography and Obituary, 58 & n.

Bailey, Samuel, *Critical Dissertation*, 1825, xv n., xvii n., xx n.
Bank restriction, 55
Blake, William
 Observations on ... the Expenditure of Government, 1823, 51–2
 Ricardo's Notes, x n.
Board of Agriculture, 50
Boswell, James, xii
Brighton, xi, 58
Buonaparte, 52

Cairnes, F. E., xii & n.
Cairnes, J. E., xii
Cambridge, University Library, xiii
Capital, and time
 creating a difference in the relative value of commodities produced by equal quantities of labour, xix & n., 12–13 (Malthus)
 See also, 47 (Malthus)
Cloth, falling in value, in contrast to corn being constant, 24–5, 27–8
Corn
 its supposedly constant value criticized, 24, 35
 when its money price increases commodities on average may not change (Malthus), 47

De Quincey, Thomas, *Dialogues*, xvii n.
Definitions in Political Economy, by Malthus, xv n.
Demand and supply (Malthus)
 and relative value, 10, 26, 37
 average state of, influence on natural value, 37
 must be restored to their universal empire, 44–5
 enter powerfully into the costs of production, 44–5
Dobb, Maurice H., ix n.
Dublin, xii & n.

Edinburgh, 53
Edinburgh Review, 58
Elba, 52
England, 22–3, 31, 38, 39, 45, 47, 48, 50, 52, 53, 54

Fixed capital
 part of it left unconsumed a component of the whole produce (Malthus), 14 & n.
 and circulating capital, 15, 40–1, their average proportion, xix n.
Free trade, 47
Funds, for the maintenance of labour, 42–3

Glut, and low prices (Malthus), 55
Grote, Mrs George, xvi n.
Gurney, Hudson, M.P., 58

Hayek, Friedrich A., xii & n.

Index

History of Economics Society Bulletin, xii n.
Hollander, J. H., xii n.
Hume, Joseph, M.P., 58 & n.
Huskisson, William, M.P., 58 & n

India, 22–3, 39, 47
International Review of Economics & Business, x n., 57 n.
Ireland, 42

James, P., *Population Malthus*, xiv n., xv n.

Keynes, Lord, xii & n.
'Keynes Papers', xii & n.
Kircudbright, 52, 53

Labour, necessary constancy of its value
  Malthus's assumption, 26, 29, 30, 31, 33, 35 (natural value), 36, 40–1, 43, criticized by Ricardo as arbitrary, 26, 29, 31, 35
  Smith's doctrine vindicated (Malthus), 32
  contrasted with constant value of the commodities produced by labour (Malthus), xiii, 43
  when its money price increases commodities on average may not change, 47
  bullion price of labour (Malthus), 49–50, 54
  See also 'Labour commanded' and 'Measure of value (value of labour as standard)'
Labour commanded
  as measure of value (Malthus), ix, xiv, xv & n., xvi, 6, 17, 19–20, 23, 41, 42, 45–6
  arbitrary as a measure, xiv, xv, xvi & n., xx, 13–14, 19, 20, 22–3, 25
  a variable measure, xvi, xx
  an extreme case, xiv
  a counterexample to Ricardo's proposition, xv
  contrasted with labour worked up or embodied, ix, xiii, xiv, xvi, xviii, 5, 23, 39, 41 n.
  a *petitio principii*, xviii & n.
  power of commanding labour, Malthus's name for value, 42–3
  whether consistently applied by Malthus, 12, 43, 48, 49
  See also 'Measure of Value (value of labour as standard)'
Labour supply, affects the value of labour, 10, 14
  changed by epidemic disease, 12 & n., 31
Landlord, whether a sufferer from tithes, 42
  largely benefited by the alterations in the value of the currency (Malthus), 55–6
Lauderdale, Earl of
  Further Considerations on the State of the Currency, 1813, 52
London School of Economics and Political Science, x n.
  at Cambridge during the war, xii & n.
London, University, xi n., 57 n.
London Magazine, xvii n.

Machinery, advantages from its use, 48
'Manuscript Revisions', by Malthus, studied by J. M. Pullen, xiv n.
McCulloch, John R., ix n., xi, xiv, xv & n., xvii n., 53, 57
  Life and Writings of David Ricardo, x, xi n.
Measure or standard of value
  its invariability, xiv, xvi, xvii, 6, 11
  never perfect, xiv, xviii, xix, xx, 8 (Malthus)
  'interminable controversy', xvi
  silver picked up in a day on the sea shore (Malthus's proposition) xvi, 19, criticized by Ricardo as a 'particular case', xviii, as an 'extreme', xix
  gold 'always the produce of the same quantity of unassisted labour' (Ricardo), xvi n.
  value of labour as standard (Malthus), xiii, xvii, 5–6, 26, 28–9, criticized by Ricardo, xvii, 9, 10–11, 12, 24–5, 26–28, 29, 31, 35, 43
  quantity of labour as standard (Ricardo), xiii, applies under the simplest form of production, 13, discussed by Malthus, 10–12, 20, not perfect due to difference, xix n., 11, difference emphasized by Malthus, 12–13, 20, 24, 32 n.
  applied to alterations in the value of the currency (Malthus), 46
  See also 'Labour commanded', 'Capital', 'Value'
Memoir of Ricardo
  its authorship established, xi n., 58 & n.
Mill, C. K., xii & n.
Mill, James, x & n., xi, xv n., xx, 9, 57
  deals with Ricardo's literary remains, x–xi & nn.
Mill, John S., xii
'Mill–Ricardo Papers', x, xi & n., xii
'Mill–Taylor Collection', x n.
Money, criterion for its value, 46
  in different countries, 21–3
Morning Chronicle, ix n., 58
Monthly Literary Advertiser, ix n.
Mure, William, of Kircudbright, an acquaintance of McCulloch's, 53

Index

Notes on Malthus, by Ricardo, 1820, x & n., xi n., xiii, xiv, xv n., xvii & n., xix n., xx, 29 n., 48 n.
Notes on Malthus's 'Measure of Value', by Ricardo, 1823
 'the only considerable item' not included in the Sraffa edn, x
 a brief sequel to the *Notes on Malthus* of 1820, xiv, xvii–xviii
 launch Ricardo into value controversy, xvi

Obergurgl, Tyrol, xii n.
O'Brien, George, xii & n.
O'Brien, D. P., 57 n.
Opere di David Ricardo, xii n.

Padua, x
Plan for the Establishment of a National Bank, by Ricardo, 1824, xi n., 58 & n.
Precious metals, as standard of value, (Malthus) 17, 20–1
 their value measured by the command of agricultural labour, 21, 23
 their value compared with labour, 46, affected by demand for corn and labour, 38
 value of gold lowered by brisk demand for corn, 48, exclusively a question of fact, 51
Profits, as an addition in the value of commodities (Malthus), xvii, 14, 15, 16, 17, 18, 30–1, 37, 44, criticized by Ricardo, 17, 19
 different effects of fall of profits on price for different classes of commodities (Malthus), 47
Proportion, of wages and profits, in value, xvii, xix, 8–9, 15, 26–7, 28–9, 39
 proportion being inverse, profits and wages cannot both rise, 29 (cp. 36)
 and command of labour, (Malthus), 27–8
 in the constant value of the variable quantity of produce which forms the wages of a given number of men, 25–6 (Malthus), 29–31, 33–4 (Malthus)
Pullen, J. M., editor of Malthus's *Principles*, xiii n., xiv n., xv n., xvi n., xix n., 16

Quarterly Review, xiii & n., 16

Real value, 15, 36 (Malthus)
Ricardo, Mrs David, xi, 58
Ricardo, Moses, David Ricardo's brother, xi, 58 & n.
'Ricardo Memorial Lectures', 57 n.
Rivista Internazionale di Scienze Economiche & Commerciali, x n., 57 n.
Royal Economic Society, xi, xii n.

Scotland, 50, 52, 53
Smith, Adam, xiii, xiv n., xviii, 5, 6 & n., 21, 30, 32, 51
 his notion of 'natural price' (Malthus), 8–9
South America, 42
Sraffa, Piero
 Ricardo's editor, ix n., x, xi & n., xii & n., xv n., xviii n., xx

'Table Illustrating the Invariable Value of Labour &c.'
 presented by Malthus, xvii & n., 32–9
Tithes, 42
Tooke, Thomas
 On High and Low Prices, 15–16, 48, 50, 51, 55
Torrens, Robert, 20
 Essay on the Production of Wealth, 1821, 14, 44
Trower, Hutches, 31 n.

United States of America, 38, 45

Value
 in use and in exchange, 7
 absolute or natural vs. nominal or relative (Malthus), 8, 18, 20–1
 natural value and natural price (Malthus), 9, 12, 21, 22–3, 33, 37–8
 constant quantity mistaken for constant value, 28–9
 and cost (Malthus), 39, 44
 of bullion, 50, 51, 52, whether lowered during the war, 48–9, 51
 See 'Labour', 'Measure or standard of value'

Wales, 54
Wants of society (Malthus), 11
Waterloo, 52
Wealth
 its close connection to value (Malthus), criticized by Ricardo, 43
Westminster Abbey, 58
Winch, Donald
 Selected Writings of James Mill, x n.

Young, Arthur
 Inquiry into the Rise of Prices in Europe, 1815, 50